For *the* Love *of* Katlyn

For *the* Love *of* Katlyn

principles and practices for a better life

Francis Alix

BIG BROWN BOOKS

Cover Photo by Jeremy Hicks
www.picsbyhicks.com
Designed by Brown & Company Design
www.browndesign.com

big brown books publishing
801 Islington Street, Suite 35, Portsmouth, NH 03801
603.436.7942

ISBN-13: 978-0692627150
www.fortheloveofkatlyn.com

Dedicated in loving memory
to my parents Ernest and Lucette.

Table of Contents

Introduction

Be the change you want to see in the world.

—Mahatma Gandhi

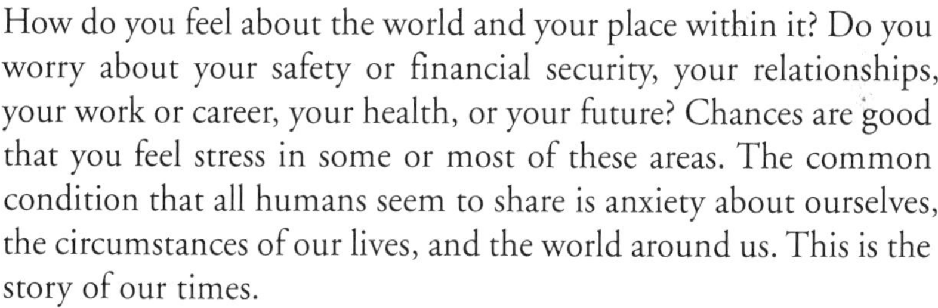

How do you feel about the world and your place within it? Do you worry about your safety or financial security, your relationships, your work or career, your health, or your future? Chances are good that you feel stress in some or most of these areas. The common condition that all humans seem to share is anxiety about ourselves, the circumstances of our lives, and the world around us. This is the story of our times.

We do not have to look far to find areas where we feel stress. We have questions about ourselves (Am I good enough?), the circumstances of our lives (Why can't I get what I want?), and the world around us (Why is there so much suffering and injustice?). Stated differently, there is a huge gap between the optimum conditions we could envision for ourselves and our world, and the conditions we observe all around us. Why is this true? What is it about the human condition that has left us individually and collectively living so far below our potential?

It seems there are certain realities about human nature at the root of this problem. Being human is complicated. Just try to observe the thoughts that run through your mind for a short period of time. Most of us experience a steady stream of desires and judgments, alternating from the regrets of the past, to happiness or negative commentary in the present, to the hopes and fears of the future. But we rarely just accept and experience the present moment with an open mind.

We also have a "higher" nature that is characterized by kindness and compassion for ourselves and others, and a "lower" nature that is characterized by judgment, selfishness, and intolerance for those who are different. Is our ability to live a better life and make the world a better place therefore limited by the reality of our lower nature, with most every man ultimately out for himself even at the expense of others?

My belief is that, even within the constraints of our human nature, there is still much we could learn about how to live better lives. I define a better life as a happier, more satisfying life, for ourselves and those we interact with. Living such a life should lead to less anxiety and more peace of mind and health of body. While we have many influences in our society that show us how to think and behave, following such direction has not reliably led us to happy, healthy or satisfying lives. In fact, observations of the world around us show that the opposite is very often true; that thinking and acting in ways that society would promote more often make us unhappy and unhealthy.

The principles and practices in this book are partly based on research on human behavior as there is a large and growing body of scientific evidence on behaviors that promote human well-being. I also draw on teachings from major cultural and religious traditions and belief systems as they collectively contain great wisdom. Throughout recorded history inspired prophets, philosophers, and others have taught us how to live our lives and create a better world. We have learned from these teachers and passed on their lessons. While their teachings about life have many common elements, and mankind has no doubt made collective progress by following them, they often diverge from one another and lead us as individuals and societies to disagreement and conflict.

Therefore, where I depart from any specific cultural or religious tradition and belief system is in my search for *universal* principles that are common among all, that can be objectively demonstrated to increase human well-being, and are supported by scientific *evidence.* This is not to imply fault with any specific faith or belief system. Quite the contrary, I offer nothing but honor and respect for the life affirming teachings of ancient religions and belief systems. But we must also recognize that some religious teachings, or perhaps more accurately the interpretation of those teachings, are not life affirming and do not increase human well-being.

It also helps to recognize that science likewise has its limitations. Science has not been able to explain many aspects of our world, such as how quantum physics works (the observation that particles that are far apart can affect each other's behavior, as though there is an invisible connection) or what dark matter is all about (that mysterious material that we can't see or detect, but seems to make up more than 80% of the universe). Science also cannot fully explain human feelings such as love and fear, or human intuition and inspiration, because they cannot be independently measured and verified. Yet all humans experience such things so they must be part of our discussion. Just as science has not developed the technology to create a human life from our raw chemical constituents, we should not expect science alone to fully inform and explain our human condition.

In searching for universal and objectively demonstrable principles to live by, my wish is that they could be accepted and applied by the largest number of people for the greatest benefit to all, including those of faith and those who are non-believers. Therefore, this book strives to be different by providing an objective examination of how we live that is grounded in research and evidence on human behaviors and their consequences, is supported by ancient religion and philosophies, but does not rely on any specific religious faith or belief system. I will also talk about my own life experiences because this is where I have learned the most about living. In discussing how to best live, we need to share our real-life experiences and the understandings we have developed over time, especially when they have come through great pain and effort. We learn best from our own experiences and observing those of others.

Another objective is to bring the great teaching of the ages into our current time, where the societal influences and life options go far beyond anything that could have been foreseen when the ancient teachings and traditions were first propagated. Therefore, there is an opportunity for ancient wisdom to be adapted to the present, updated by knowledge gained from scientific research on human behavior, and then applied in a manner that provides meaningful guidance in our current life context.

My final objective involves individual and collective healing. Early in the process of writing this book, I experienced what is every parent's worst nightmare. My 25-year-old daughter, Katlyn, took her own life. I came upon the scene as the emergency medical team was trying to revive her, went to her side and held her as they worked on her, praying for her to come back to us. But somehow I knew she would not be returning. Katlyn's suicide is still incomprehensible to me. I had no warning at all and would not have foreseen the possibility in a million years. The pain is still fresh and each day my heart breaks anew as I shed endless tears for her loss.

Katlyn was born 30 minutes after my 32nd birthday ended, forever my special gift from above. She was the love of my life, the most beautiful and precious little bundle I had ever seen. Her light shined brightly from the start. Katlyn was irresistible. She was a force of nature. When I came home from work she would scream "Daddy, Daddy, Daddy" and crash into me at the doorway, wrapping her arms around my legs and squeezing them with all her might.

The memories of Katlyn's brilliance flood my mind. She had more than a spark; she lit up the room. And she had a heart of gold. She cared about everyone, especially those put down by others. In grade school she sought out the unpopular kids and made them her friend so they would not feel outcast or unworthy. In high school and college, she would not join the cliques because she refused to put people down and wanted to be friends with everyone. Because of her compassion for the less fortunate and her strength and independence she sometimes had trouble with peers which deeply pained her.

Below is one of the many beautiful tributes to Katlyn left by a childhood friend:

I don't know many people in the world that I can truly say have the purest heart, that are effortlessly kind, always a wonderful person to be around, and a loyal, loving friend. You helped me through some of the hardest times of my life and we grew up together. This is the definition of tragedy for all of us... but I know having you as an angel is a true blessing on its own. I love you Katlyn Alix and will forever remember all of the years we spent together.

How do I make sense of the loss of Katlyn who was such a beautiful person who had positively impacted so many? I am still struggling hard to find answers to this question. With her huge and fragile heart, she often took on the problems and struggles of others, while the injustices she faced personally just piled up. Those like Katlyn, who are such a loving and healing presence for others, are often that way because they carry the deepest wounds. And they are frequently the ones in greatest need of healing.

So in writing this book I have the secondary objective of honoring Katlyn and sharing the lessons I am learning from this tragedy. It has become abundantly clear to me that expressing and healing our existing emotional wounds is a critical part of having a better life. Personal change is deeply rooted in both better understanding and emotional healing. I am devastated over the reality that we were not able to bring this healing to Katlyn, but because of her loss I am also committed to do everything in my power to help others learn from this tragedy and receive the emotional healing they need.

Therefore, I ask your permission to enter into this dialogue with you with the hope of finding common ground on a set of principles on how to live that could be applied broadly to reduce our anxiety and improve our lives. I also ask you to allow me to talk about my life experiences and my little Katlyn's life—how she lived it with passion and commitment, and how emotional healing could have helped her stay with us. My hope is that Katlyn's example may help you or a loved one relieve emotional suffering and gain the better life that you desire and deserve.

My final objective is to propose a daily practice to apply these principles in our lives in the hopes that our world could become a better place. This goal may sound utopian, but I believe the condition of our personal lives and the world around us is a reflection of our individual and collective knowledge, experience, and choices. Armed with a better understanding and universal truths about how to live a better life, in addition to a practice to apply them, the change we seek becomes possible. But societal change starts at the personal level, and so we must begin as individuals. As the great Indian philosopher Mahatma Gandhi said, "Be the change that you want to see in the world."

A Word of Love and Caution

If you feel so unworthy or your challenges in life are so great that you question your ability to go on living, you need more help than this book can provide. Please accept that no matter how intense is your pain, it is possible to find some relief. Despair is created in our minds and with the right help we can feel safe again and begin to see things differently. If you are like Katlyn you have kept your feelings of unworthiness and doubts about living to yourself out of shame or not wanting to upset anyone. This makes your problems appear much worse than they really are.

When we keep our problems locked up inside, our mind can spiral downward in depression and despair because there is no one to help us see a different perspective. I was never given the chance to see the depth of Katlyn's suffering and I am certain that I could have helped her feel safe again and get the help she needed to see things differently. Her loss was so tragic and unnecessary. So please, for the love of my sweet Katlyn, accept that it is possible to find relief for the suffering you experience and go to a friend, family member, hospital, doctor, therapist or call a suicide hotline and ask for help as soon as possible. And if you have a friend or family member who might fit this description, please see that they do the same.

Chapter 1

Why are We Here?

In the end, it's not the years in your life that count. It's the life in your years.

—Abraham Lincoln

If you consider yourself happy you are more likely a young or old person. Research shows that feelings of happiness follow a U-shaped curve throughout our lives, with peaks in our earliest and later years. The surprising evidence shows that in all societies feelings of happiness and well-being decrease throughout our adult lives until they bottom out somewhere around mid-life (mid 40's in the United States) when they finally start to improve again. If you are fortunate enough to live into your 60s and 70s, chances are good that you'll end up feeling happier than when you were a teenager.

All this seems counterintuitive when you consider that most of us were anxious to grow up to enjoy the freedom and power of adulthood and dreaded the idea of growing old because we thought we would become much less capable and limited. So what is the cause of this increasingly depressing, then eventually improving and ultimately satisfying journey through life? What is it that life teaches us? What changes for us? Do we change personally, or do our life circumstances change, or both?

Let's start at the beginning. Have you thought about why you are here on earth or, "Why am I doing what I am doing?" It would be difficult to develop principles for how to live without first asking this question. Our physical arrival into this world is based on the choices of other human beings who join to create our new life. The circumstances of our birth are not in our control. And as an infant whether or not we survive is also out of our control. We are completely dependent on our parents or caretakers for survival. So figuring out why we are here and what we want out of life necessarily comes later.

Survival is our most basic human instinct. This is true for all animals. Human survival requires air, nutrition, shelter from the environment, and physical nurturing. When an infant does not receive enough of these he or she cries or screams. As we age we learn to communicate our wants and needs directly. We discover we have choices, and that certain choices result in more positive outcomes and other choices more negative. We may still cry and scream as adults when we don't get what we want, as this pattern is part of human nature that does not have to be taught.

After survival needs are met much of humankind takes their purpose for living directly from religions or belief systems regarding a life after death. In the West, religions teach a belief in a loving creator God and a set of behaviors that lead to a closer connection to Him and a magnificent afterlife with God defined as heaven. Christians, Muslims, and Jews all come from the same religious lineage and share these same basic beliefs. They teach that following their religions should lead to a better life on earth as well as an extraordinary afterlife in heaven.

I was raised as a Roman Catholic and attended a Catholic high school. My early experience with religion was positive and I benefited from witnessing the humble devotion to God and family demonstrated by my parents. Their loving example helped me to become a more kind and giving person. This is not meant to be an endorsement for the Christian faith in general or Catholicism specifically, or a judgment against any other religion or belief system, including those of non-believers, but only a sharing of my upbringing and early experience with religion.

In the East, belief systems such as Hinduism and Buddhism are focused on a path to connect with the Universal Spirit or mind of all creation, of which they believe we are all part. Through their prescribed practices, they teach that humans are able to transcend suffering and achieve an enlightened consciousness or a state of liberation where we lose our separate identity and come into union with this Universal Spirit. The major Eastern religions also believe that our individual soul experiences rebirth in a series of successive lives in order to continue our spiritual path and eventually reach enlightenment or liberation.

For me, the Universal Spirit recognized in the Eastern belief systems along with the state called enlightenment or liberation (i.e. oneness with all of creation) has similarities with the creator God recognized in Western religions and the place called heaven (i.e. oneness with the creator God). The differences between them might be explained by semantics. The spiritual truths revealed by our Master teachers like Jesus, Buddha, Krishna, Muhammad, Confucius, Moses, and others could be different perspectives of the same truth. The sacred scriptures were most often written many generations after the Master teacher had died and interpreted according to local cultures. It is generally accepted that the scripture writers did not have the level of understanding and connection to the Divine that the Master teachers had. Therefore, we should expect differences even if the Masters were all teaching the same basic truths. Gandhi perhaps demonstrated this understanding best. When asked if he was a Hindu, he said, *Yes I am. I am also a Muslim, a Christian, a Buddhist, and a Jew.*

Pope Francis, the leader of the Catholic Church, offered this perspective about mankind in relation to God and religion:

It is not necessary to believe in God to be a good person. In a way, the traditional notion of God is outdated. One can be spiritual but not religious. It is not necessary to go to church and give money - for many, nature can be a church. Some of the best people in history did not believe in God, while some of the worst deeds were done in His name.

Some may be tempted to dismiss thoughts of religion altogether in a book like this. However, a large majority of the world's population (84%) holds some type of religious belief, with Christianity (32%), Islam (23%), and Hinduism (15%) being the top three. Even among the estimated 16% of the world's people who have no religious affiliation, about half of those still hold some religious or spiritual beliefs, such as belief in God or a Universal spirit, but do not identify with a specific faith. Therefore, a serious look at how to live our lives should consider these religious and spiritual beliefs and seek a common ground from which the vast majority of us would be comfortable.

Science also has much to say about our purpose for life based on the study of human nature. Abraham Maslow discussed the human hierarchy of needs and motivations in his 1943 paper "A Theory of Human Motivation." He recognized our survival needs as the most basic ones that must first be satisfied for continuation of life. He next prioritized the need for safety and security which includes personal safety, financial security, and health security, as second level motivators. This makes sense as once we have met our basic needs for survival it is clear that remaining free from harm and disease, and having the capability to provide for our physiological needs on a continuing basis (i.e. financial security), would take priority as a basic purpose for life.

Maslow's next level of human needs involve love and belonging as humans need to feel loved and have a sense of acceptance in their family and among social groups. We know from personal experience that our need for love and acceptance is a powerful motivator. So powerful, in fact, that infants and newborn animals that don't feel this love and sense of parental connection from birth often cannot survive, or become emotionally disabled. Therefore, love and belonging appear to be a more basic survival need, at least from birth into early childhood. In some circumstances humans will even neglect their own survival for the love of another. Military and law enforcement personnel risk this type of sacrifice every day.

After the need for survival, security, and love and belonging are met, Maslow suggests that the need for self-esteem and self-expression are our primary motivations. The need for self-esteem can be seen through our work or other activities that provide the opportunity for accomplishment and help us gain the respect of others. Self-expression, or "self-actualization" in Maslow's words, refers to the desire to realize our full potential and express our highest calling in life. The modern world has created seemingly unlimited opportunities for the pursuit of self-esteem and self-expression, so the idea that humans are motivated by these needs also appears evident.

While the theory of human needs and motivations is interesting and informative when asking what our purpose is in life, what can we observe in the world around us today, and what can we conclude from these observations about why we are here? There is a large portion of the world's population that is primarily concerned with their needs for survival and security. They may live under constant physical threat, have no reliable source of clean water or food, are subjected to sickness or disease with little or no healthcare resources, and often have no stable shelter or home. Many of these people live in city ghettos or war torn regions and have no means or ability to relocate. Without a change in their life circumstances, which is often completely out of their control, they have little hope for a better life.

For these unfortunate people who are usually born into such an existence, their survival needs dominate their lives and their most basic desire is not for happiness as we might think of it, but simply having their survival and security needs met. This raises an obvious question of human justice. Why should they be destined to a life of suffering for survival just because of the circumstances of their birth, while many others have wealth that is thousands of times greater than they need, largely because of different birth circumstances? We should not be surprised, therefore, by the embedded anger and violence in these areas. We know there are enough resources produced on this planet to provide for the basic survival and security needs of all humans. Therefore, this is a problem of basic human compassion and justice that needs to be addressed if we collectively wish to live in a better world.

For most of us who live in the developed world our survival needs are met, with our safety and security for the most part assured, and with our basic education and health care needs provided. However, the need for acceptance and belonging has been more difficult for us to meet as our modern culture has become more fragmented and individualistic. The close neighborhoods and strong communities common in our past have largely been lost. Our contemporary need for belonging is often expressed by an obsession with television, the internet, email, text, Facebook, and tweet communications regarding all manner of thoughts and experiences that arise in each moment. We can also find support on the internet and cable television for almost any extreme view that one could contemplate—views which often prey on our prejudices and fears to recruit followers. Despite this significant increase in communications of our age, enabled by powerful and inexpensive telecommunications technology, surveys indicate that overall humans have never felt more lonely. The personal connection and sense of belonging that we are after is not satisfied by the modern world we live in.

Our society has also developed many options for gaining self-esteem or self-expression. It promotes the attainment of a multitude of life objectives such as wealth, fame, power, status, beauty, excess material goods, exciting entertainment, and pleasure. The opportunities to pursue such ends are for all practical purposes unlimited. With all of these options being promoted and pursued in the developed world an obvious question would be—why? Why should I want power, wealth, fame, excess material goods, or a near constant digital communication with others? What am I really after or what basic need am I trying to satisfy? Is this really about self-esteem or expression or is some other more basic need motivating us, such as desire for love and acceptance?

People who have their basic needs satisfied would likely respond that they are looking for happiness and acceptance or perhaps trying to express or prove themselves. For most of us, the feeling of happiness or acceptance is a momentary event that arises from our immediate life circumstances, and then slowly falls away. It is based on "getting what we want" in that moment, and when we are no longer getting what we want, or we encounter something we don't like, our feeling of happiness vanishes. Our life circumstances, like our personal relationships, go up and down. Is our happiness necessarily tied to them?

Beyond the desire for happiness and acceptance, any attempt to express ourselves or prove our self-worth based on wealth, status, power, appearance, or material attainment is a never ending quest for more, and bigger, and better stuff, simply because it is not possible to measure up to the perfect ideals that society places before us. We can never have "the most" or be "the best" and "most beautiful," other than on a limited, relative basis. Even if this were possible, it would only be for a moment, as someone else would soon have more or be better. Additionally, we are all going to grow older and die, and "you can't take any of that with you," as the saying goes, so what's the point?

Where does this leave us regarding our primary purpose for living, once our needs for survival and security are met? Religions and belief systems provide a compelling purpose for life for many people. Though they are not entirely consistent with one another, there are certain principles that are common to all religions such as "love thy neighbor," for example, which can lead to a better life and do not depend on belief in an afterlife. But even those who embrace the teachings of religion or other belief systems may still search for greater happiness and expression and less stress and anxiety. If we follow the influences of modern society in this search, are we just striving in vain for the unattainable and setting ourselves up to fail? This appears to be so, but I don't believe it is necessary. There are better alternatives.

There is a growing body of research on human happiness and well-being that has come from a branch of the social sciences called Positive Psychology. Martin Seligman at the University of

Pennsylvania (Penn) is one of its founders. His published works on the topic include *Authentic Happiness* and *Flourish*. Seligman was the first to suggest that psychology should seek to understand and treat more than human suffering in the form of depression, addiction, trauma, or other mental health affliction. He suggested that psychology also needed to understand what makes life worth living and what creates well-being because with this understanding we could proactively work to create the enabling conditions for human "flourishing," like we would help a plant flourish by giving it sufficient sunlight, water, and nutrients.

Seligman has developed a theory of well-being, which he defines as having five elements: *positive emotion* (happiness or peace of mind), *engagement* (feeling of being absorbed in something), *meaning* (serving something larger than the self), *positive relationships* (people who really care about us), and *accomplishment* (success at life's chosen activities). He collectively refers to these well-being attributes as "PERMA" and if we look at them individually they are completely consistent with religious beliefs, but do not depend upon them. He and his colleagues at Penn have also developed a series of tests and practices that can be used to identify our particular human strengths and to learn or reinforce behaviors that increase happiness and well-being.

The work of Seligman and others like him in positive psychology is particularly valuable as the conclusions they reach are grounded in the discipline of science, using carefully administered surveys and tests that sometimes produce insights contrary to conventional beliefs or ancient wisdom. They provide the "objective evidence" of what really helps us live better lives. I will refer back to this research later in this book.

I conducted some limited personal research on the purpose of life with a few people that I believed were leading exemplary lives. I interviewed my mother on this question in February 2013, around her 90th birthday. My mom was a devout Catholic who attended Mass every day when there were no young children at home and she could still drive a car. She, along with my father, raised thirteen of us healthy and happy children (yes, that number is correct!). I am number seven of thirteen children, with six boys and seven girls in my family. In response to my questions about the purpose of life, my mother offered, *God created human life so we could share heaven with Him forever.* Her personal life goal was to *get together with Him in heaven.* She went on to say, *Life is what you make of it with your own free will. My life has been very, very good. My education could not have been better. My family is so, so good.*

When I asked her who or what were her greatest influences in teaching her how to live, she said it was her parents and her schoolteachers. Her teachers were primarily Catholic as my mother attended only Catholic schools up to and including Catholic University in Washington, DC.

When I asked my Mom what, if anything, she needed to be happier with her life, she said *Only Heaven could make me happier. I spent my whole life serving others. Jesus said those who serve will be first, so I am all set.* Even with that faith, she also said, *I need to pray more and stay in tune with what God wants for me, although I have no clue what it is.*

Hearing her say that she had "no clue" what God wants for her at first seemed strange to me. But over time I have come to believe that her response indicated that she was wondering why she hadn't already gone to heaven. She had come close to death a year earlier and gotten a glimpse of heaven, so I think this was a lingering question for her. She had lost most of her mobility and was constantly attended to by others, which was the opposite of how she had lived her life. My mother made her way to heaven less than a year later in January 2014. As her family and friends, we lost a beautiful and loving a soul, but at the same time she gained the reward she worked for her whole life.

I interviewed another friend, Bill Wetzel, who was one of my graduate school professors. Our relationship had grown over the years to where he became not only one of my best friends, but also like a second father to me. He is the kindest, most thoughtful person I have ever known, aside from my parents, and I knew that he had no religious affiliation. Like my parents, Bill was something of a local legend in that everyone who knew him loved him and looked up to him. For those of us lucky enough to call him a friend, his life was a shining example to follow. Being a part of the same generation as my parents and living a similar life of kindness, compassion, and service to others, I was anxious to see how his answers might differ from my mother's as all of her thoughts and actions were based on a deep faith in God.

When I mentioned the idea of this book to Bill he was very enthusiastic as he felt there was a real need. He thought my greatest challenge would be *getting the message out to others with all the media noise that exists.* He thought video games that show role playing, with real life choices and their different consequences, could be a great way to teach children. Bill's first response showed he was still fundamentally a teacher at heart and had a lot of contemporary awareness for a man in his eighties.

When I asked Bill, based on his experience, what leads to a happy life, he said, *First I want security, then I want to help others, then I want to make a contribution or a difference in the world.* He went on to say he had no real material wants. He did not need power, but he did want to control certain aspects of his own life. Bill's ideas of what leads to a happy life is quite consistent with Maslow's hierarchy of motivators and needs. It is also fascinating how much Bill's fundamental desire to serve others parallels my mother's, even though she had a very different motivation. This helps support the idea that there may be fundamental principles to live by that could help all of us live better lives, believers and non-believers alike. Subscribing to a specific religion or belief system may be helpful, but does not appear necessary to live a happy, meaningful, and fulfilling life.

I also interviewed Katlyn in February of 2013, when she was twenty-three and less than one year out of college. When I asked her the purpose of human life, she said, *I don't know.* When I asked who or what were the major influences on teaching her how to live, she responded, *My parents, brothers, Catholic high school, friends, and social media.* When I asked Katlyn what she needed to be happier, she responded, *I need to be happier with myself. I need to love myself a lot more. That's the biggest thing I need and then everything else will fall into place.*

I asked Katlyn what the world needed to become a better place and she responded, *Empathy, more even distribution of the world's resources and wealth, acceptance of other people and their way of life, more stewardship of the earth. There's like a million billion things. Improve mental health care facilities and prisons; improve education. Make it so every country can meet basic needs so people are able to better their own lives. Poverty is more of a choice, not the only option.*

I asked her how she needed to change, if at all, to be happier and she said there were *too many things to respond to that question.* I asked who she most admired and why. She said *Jesus* and *just because,* then added her *family, dad, mom, and brothers.*

Finally Katlyn offered this observation on the world that she experienced, which provides a window into her personal suffering.

Everything today is focused about yourself—me, me, me. People just don't notice anything about anyone else unless it impacts them. Everything is about their own personal desires, needs, and convenience. No one really thinks of others. College group projects were so hard because no one knows how to consider others. If you are not taught to think about others by your parents or church, you are not going to learn it because society teaches you just to think of yourself. I avoid people who intentionally do things to hurt others—just write them off. At my job I was always helping out because we were a team, but no one else would do that. All they did was trash talk others, customers, and complain. No one really gets it.

Katlyn, however, did seem to "get it." One of her best friends wrote this:

A sweet soul taken from us way too soon. My heart hurts today thinking about the loss of such an amazing person and friend. Katlyn could put a smile on anyone's face and could light up a room when she walked in. Words can't express how much I am going to miss this sweet girl. I will always cherish the memories we've had. I only wish that we had time to make more. May you rest in peace and forever be in our hearts.

This chapter began with the question "Why are we here and what is our purpose?" Based upon the available teachings, the scientific research, and the observations we can make, there may be as many answers to that question as there are individuals on earth. My mother had a definitive answer to the question based on her faith in God while Bill had a similar answer, but did not share her faith in God. Katlyn just said, "I don't know." However, my mother, Katlyn, and Bill were all longing for a more loving and kind world and lived their lives accordingly, trying to be of loving service to others. For me, this points us in a direction we need to further explore.

We have all been taught about how to live our lives, and indirectly about its purpose, since we were children. We have probably learned more from the examples of those around us than from any specific teachings they may have shared. Parents and teachers today may not have the influence that they once did, as children are exposed to many more influences than in the past and parents on average are less available and present for their children. In filling this "parental and institutional void" in teaching our children how to live, our modern society and culture sends confusing messages at best, and deeply damaging ones at worst.

What we know is that we are human and there are needs we all share such as desires for survival, security, love and belonging, accomplishment, and self-expression. This provides at least a partial answer of why we are here. We can explore those basic human needs along with the teachings of ancient wisdom and modern science to develop a set of universal principles and practices that help us better meet our own hopes and desires for a happy and fulfilling life. This is true even if our primary focus is to get to heaven or achieve enlightenment.

We started out this chapter with the research finding that human happiness follows a U-shaped curve during our lives, bottoming out around midlife, and finally peaking in our old age if we are lucky enough to get there. One cause of this phenomenon is that we are not taught basic principles on how to live in order to achieve happiness and well-being. Instead, what we are taught often leads us in the opposite direction. We can continue our slow process of learning how to be happy through life experiences and the mistakes we make and correct over time. Or we could take a more active role right now in discerning the best way to live and as a result, maybe get to happiness a little sooner.

Katlyn showed it was possible to put an amazing amount of *life in your years*, as Abe Lincoln would say, so let's not be satisfied with less. It is my sincere wish that the discussion and recommended practice that follows can be of value in that regard to believers and non-believers alike, and thereby help us individually and collectively create a better life right now, and move our world closer together.

Chapter 2

Love and Kindness

I need to be happier with myself.
I need to love myself a lot more.
That's the biggest thing I need and
then everything else will fall into place.

—Katlyn Alix

I did not realize at the time how well this comment above, from my Katlyn when she was only twenty-three years old, summed up one of the most important pieces of wisdom that we need to start with in the process of healing and learning to live a better life. When Katlyn was in high school and struggling with her romantic relationship of several years, I told her that she could not expect her boyfriend to make her happy, and that no one can do that for someone else. I said that we need to learn to love ourselves first.

I remember Katlyn looking at me at the time like my statement was nonsense. I could see our discussion was going nowhere. Now as I reread her comment above I guess my words did not fall on deaf ears after all. But this is a terribly hard lesson to learn, as we come into this world completely dependent on our parents for love and we carry that same paradigm of looking for love outside of ourselves for the rest of our lives, or at least until the pain of failure points us in a new direction.

It wasn't until after I had my own children that I really began to understand this. Coming from such a large family, I was the baby for about one year and 4 months, then my little brother came along and I moved to priority number two. This process of gaining a new sibling was repeated five more times before I was ten years old, each time moving me further back in the "parental love and attention" queue. I am not complaining as I was fortunate to come from such a large and loving family. But this family dynamic had consequences for my early childhood development that took some time for me to realize.

Even with parents as loving and devoted as mine, their ability to offer love and attention was limited primarily to the baby. Dad worked in his own auto service shop, 9am-9pm, 6-7 days a week, to provide for us. Mom worked about sixteen hours a day, 6-7 days a week, for the entire time I lived at home. Just cooking, cleaning, shopping, and doing laundry for all of us was such an overwhelming responsibility, to say nothing of watching the young ones that were not yet in school. I still don't know how she did it. The older children surely helped out with the younger ones, but it is a miracle that we all grew up healthy and functional.

I remember being both happy and sad growing up. My brothers, sisters, and I had a lot of fun playing games we invented and getting into mischief. But we inevitably fought over things, and the outcome of our fights was usually determined by the largest and strongest among us. That was frequently not me, as I had six older brothers and sisters. The common admonition to me when I was hurt by an older sibling was "don't be such a baby." I used the same phrase on my younger siblings when I hurt them. In hindsight, this seems so ironic because deep inside "the baby" is probably what all of us longed to be, at least from a parental love and attention perspective. My older brother once told me that the most vivid memory he had of my Mom growing up was a picture of her back working over the stove, sink, washer, etc.

My mother did not have time to referee for us. She would tell us to fight our own battles, or stay away from your brother or sister if you don't want to get hurt. To her credit, I never heard her raise her voice once, another miracle from my perspective. When things got out of hand, she would calmly spank whichever one of us she thought was most responsible or threaten to get our Dad, who was working at the garage just down the hill. That threat was usually enough to stop any commotion in its tracks.

My mom's approach to discipline often did not work out well for me, as I tended to be more rambunctious than many of my siblings and seemed to always be getting myself in trouble. From my perspective, I got no relief when my older siblings hurt me, as though I deserved it, which I probably did. But when I picked on my younger siblings, justice seemed to come to me swiftly and efficiently.

I remember an occasion when I was sent to my room after a spanking and I just cried my eyes out, wondering why my mother and everyone else hated me. This was not a momentary emotional question for me, but one that remained deep inside for much of my childhood. I used to think there was something wrong with me because my brothers and sisters did not seem to suffer this way (although looking back, they may have). I even asked my mother why she hated me. When I look now at pictures taken of the family between my ages of 6-11 years old, I am always looking down at the ground as though I didn't feel worthy to be in the picture or the family.

The result was that in navigating the painful jungle of sibling relationships that was my childhood proving ground, I became quite clever and tough, at least externally. This was just a basic survival mechanism that I developed. As I went off to school, I realized that I had capabilities and a maturity beyond my years when compared to my peers. I felt like my classmates acted so much younger than me. This allowed me to make friends and succeed in social situations more easily than in my family. And with this new reality in school my confidence grew. I still got in trouble at times, but my bold behavior at school only made my classmates look up to me, so in a real sense I was winning the love and attention that I craved.

After school, like most of my older siblings, I was in a rush to get married and start a family of my own, which for me happened one year after college graduation. I think we older children all suffered from a parental love and attention deficit, and finding someone who loves you enough to marry you felt like a good remedy at the time. Having a child would also allow me to experience that close bond between a parent and child that I had missed growing up. Therefore, my early desire for marriage and children is understandable looking back. But there were several problems in the way I approached this part of my life that would only be revealed later.

Once I did have a child, as I said at the beginning of the chapter, I began to understand myself better. My first son was born when I was twenty-four years old and it was a completely life-changing experience. He was amazing and energetic from the start. I remember the doctor saying he was one of the most beautiful infants he had ever seen. I also remember bursting with love and wonderment at his arrival. Like all babies, he grew up attached to his parents and entertained us with his love and laughter. This bond was very healing for me, as I began to realize this was an intimate loving relationship that I had sorely missed as a child.

My son turned out to be more like me than I expected, especially when it came to mischief. He was completely charming and disarming to everyone he met, and really still is, but he was easily bored and had a strong independent streak. As a result, he would often do other than what he was told, which was challenging for us as parents. And when he misbehaved, we did what we were taught to do, which was to raise our voice at him, spank him, or otherwise punish him by sending him to his room.

It did not take long to see how this crushed my son's spirit and made him lash out even more. I saw myself in his pain and rejection. I realized he was only being himself and he just wanted to be loved, to express his true nature, and have some fun. Seeing his little heart break made my heart break and led me to be more accepting of him and forgiving of his transgressions. He was still that pure and innocent child that I first fell in love with.

It was at this point that I began to understand that I too just wanted to be loved, more than anything else. That is all I had wanted as a child. When I acted out as a child, it was all about getting the love and attention I needed. And everything I was doing in life at that moment, my marriage and family, my relationships, my work and outside activities were all based on gaining the love and approval that I still felt lacking. I always had something to prove. Now I realized that what I was trying to prove is that I was worthy—worthy of being loved.

Isn't this true most everywhere we look? Why do so many people strive for power, wealth, and fame? Some amount of money and power, at least enough to have control of our own lives, is desirable for all of us. But the extreme wealth, power, and fame glamorized in the media and sought by so many must have another motivation. It is clear that they have something to prove as well. These external achievements boost our self-image as they are used by society to judge our worth. When we obtain these things, we get the approval or even adulation of others. We have thereby "proved" our greatness, at least by the standards of the modern world. Alternatively, if we love and accept ourselves just as we are, there is nothing left to prove and no reason to strive for such things to gain approval of others. Then wealth, fame, and power would be desirable only to the extent they could be used to help others.

My observations and those of social science suggest that this condition, of looking outside ourselves for love and acceptance, is nearly universal. Maslow's theory states the need for love and belonging is second only to our survival instincts. Those who do not feel this underlying motivation may not yet have discovered their innermost desires, as it took some time for me to realize how important this was. Our human defense and coping mechanisms are quite capable of building a self-story of wellness and strength even around a deep wound. I know as I was particularly skilled at this.

If you were fortunate enough to have loving and accepting parents, were born with a bright mind and athletic talent so you did well in school, and even have attractive physical features so you have no problem gaining the affection of others, you may feel pretty good about yourself even in a world of conditional love and acceptance. Still there is something of value in understanding others who are less fortunate because this is the real world for the majority of us. One day the less fortunate person you need to understand may be your child, sibling, or friend. I suspect that even those who look like they are on top of the world are still insecure and terribly afraid that someone or something will come along to knock them off.

A few years ago, I saw a TV program featuring the pop music star Christina Aguilera on *VH-1 Storytellers*, filmed in 2010. She discussed the story behind her hit song, *Beautiful.* The songwriter, Linda Perry, talked about how she was extremely insecure growing up, always being told she was not good enough, not pretty enough, not smart enough. People eventually made her feel ugly and worthless. When Christina heard the song, she immediately identified with it and wanted to record it, even though no one would think that a beautiful and successful pop star like Christina could harbor such feelings. Her passion for this song came through with her emotional declaration: *I am beautiful, no matter what they say, cause words can't bring me down. I am beautiful, in every single way, cause words can't bring me down. Don't you bring me down today.*

Let's walk through a typical child's upbringing and see how this feeling of not being good enough is created. We start again with the helpless infant who needs a parent's love and nurturing to survive. Imagine you are in the presence of someone who makes you feel beautiful, amazing, even perfect, and there is not one thing they would change about you. This is what we normally experience as an infant. Our parents are accepting of our crying and neediness because they know we don't know any better and therefore can do nothing else. Our parents smile and "coo" at us, tell us how cute we are, and attend to our every need. But once we grow into a child and learn to communicate with our parents, this dynamic changes.

Our parents then start to set expectations around our behavior to the extent that we can understand them.

Invariably, there comes a time, or a great number of times, when a young child willfully disobeys the parent or reacts with great emotion when they don't get what they want. In fact, we identify that time in the early child's life as the "Terrible Twos" to distinguish when this rebellious behavior kicks in at around two years of age. If we think of what the young child experiences when they are first told they cannot have what they want or are told what they are doing is wrong, this must feel like a total rejection. They are just expressing their true nature and normal human desires, and then WHAM!, *there goes the love that I need for survival.* No wonder they have a tantrum.

For a child, these are very influential moments. Because they are completely dependent on their parents, there is nothing more important than feeling safe. For them, safe equates to food and love. And taking away love means the same as taking away food, certain death. This is literally true, because no child can survive on his or her own. Even though most of us do not carry this conscious awareness with us after childhood, deep inside we fear the loss of love as much as any other threat. So, we need to hold the child in these moments and help them feel safe again.

A child no doubt needs to learn boundaries and acceptable behavior, both to protect himself from harm and to get along with others. We need to learn early in life that our actions have consequences. Even though these difficult learning moments for the child are unavoidable, we can still approach him or her with sensitivity to their need for our love and acceptance. My suggestion for parents based on this awareness is to offer a correction to your child as kindly and gently as possible, and assure your child that you still love and accept him or her. They are not being "bad"—they are just being "human"—and you are not rejecting them in any way. The correction is to help you, them, and others be happier and get along better, and your love and affection for them remains as strong as ever. It is obvious that most of us did not experience this type of loving discipline as children.

Nevertheless we do not want to judge our parents. They probably treated us more gently and lovingly than they were treated by their own parents. And what did they learn when they were disciplined by raised voices, spanking, or other forms of punishment, accompanied by the idea that they were being bad? This sent a couple of troubling messages. The first is that you should do as you are expected because if you don't, you will lose your parent's love and approval. The discipline they received was based on fear. In other words, *My love for you is based upon your behavior. When you behave incorrectly, you will receive no love because you are not worthy of being loved. So you better do what you're told or else.*

Secondly, by example of our parents' conditional love and acceptance, and the punishment they meted out to us, we learned that withholding love and punishing others is what you do when they don't meet your expectations. I struck my younger brother when I was angry with him, just as I was struck by my parents and older siblings. I too learned to discipline others based on fear and knew just how to apply it. And so it goes, from generation to generation. This may sound harsh, but it is surely what most of us learned as we can see it all around us, in our world and in our relationships. I don't deny that the use of fear to motivate behaviors can be effective. It is endorsed by most all cultures and religions. However, there may be a better approach that is equally or more effective and doesn't result in the unwanted consequences of emotional wounds and low self-esteem.

Our educational experience reinforces this feeling that we are not worthy. In school, we are judged and graded for everything we do academically, athletically, and socially. We are rewarded when we are at the top of the class, treated like nothing special when we are in the middle, and punished when we are at the bottom. For eighty-percent or more of students, this does not help their self-esteem. This reward and punishment phenomenon exists with both teachers and students. Katlyn spoke to me of "mean girls" that would form a clique of only the most popular girls, then trash talk those who were not worthy in their judgment, and punish anyone who dared to cross them. She resisted these cliques out of love and compassion for those who were rejected and suffered the cliques' punishment as a result. This caused her a lot of pain.

We grow up with these primary influences at home and school, and learn that we should spend our lives trying to meet the expectations of our families, friends, boyfriends or girlfriends, partners, spouses, social groups, religious leaders, supervisors-peers at work, and modern society. And like it or not, most of us do not measure up, at least in our own minds. When we look outside of ourselves for love and approval, it poses an underlying question of our self-worth. And when we fail to get the love and acceptance we desire, our self-worth suffers. The truth is that the sheer number of outside demands and influences ensure that we could never measure up. How could we possibly live up to so many explicit and implicit expectations?

As a result, in the developed world at least, we are terribly insecure. Though we may not be aware, most all of us harbor feelings of not being good enough. We experience this as near constant anxiety or lingering doubt about ourselves. Our insecurity may also manifest with pride or outward shows of confidence, but it all comes down to the same questions of self-worth. On top of doubts about our worthiness is the reality that our world is becoming increasingly complex and interdependent, which only increases our insecurity. The more complex the world, the harder for us to understand how to function within it, the more insecure we are about our prospects for success. As the world grows in interdependence, we are also individually growing in insecurity, which taken together is a frightening trend. For many, life feels like a house of cards that could come tumbling down or explode at any moment. And the problem is not getting any better.

Confronted with fragmented families and social structures along with unprecedented pressure from their schools, extracurricular activities, and social media, the younger generation suffers from this insecurity to a much larger extent than their parents. Our modern society provides them with unmeetable expectations, unrealistic body images, shows little if any examples of positive human values, and celebrates standards of success and material wealth that are obtainable only by the few. They learn that life is all about themselves, as Katlyn would say, and this leads to interpersonal conflict. The organizations that promote these views are motivated by their own financial gains, not our well-being. Katlyn felt increasing levels of stress and anxiety over our modern culture as she made her way out into the world. The dramatically increasing use of antidepressant medication among our youth demonstrates this truth.

Thus, our choices in life normally revolve around trying to meet the expectations of others in attempts to please them and gain their love and approval, even though for most of us this is a losing cause. At the same time, we judge and punish those that fail to meet our own expectations. Whether or not those choices and judgments lead to a more satisfying or fulfilling life is a secondary concern because this is what we were taught from early childhood onward and this is what we know to do. Once we recognize this pattern for what it is and realize that no one is to blame for this, there is a possibility for greater understanding, and then compassion, and then healing. And with that comes the ability to make a different choice.

How do we make a different choice? How do we learn to love ourselves when there are so many things we experience that remind us that we are not good enough? You might expect that because I am writing this book, I must have the answer. I wish it were that simple. I can speak of my own experience, but I must confess, learning to love myself is still a work in progress. After discussing my own experience, I'll review what ancient wisdom and modern science have to say about our need for love and how and where we might find it.

Learning to love myself started after my failed marriage when I had to face my extreme guilt and feelings of unworthiness. This was the point where I hit bottom. I was so confused because I loved my children more than anything in life. But I believed my relationship with my wife was so dysfunctional that it was actually hurting my children more to see us together than it would if we were apart. So I left the home where the ones I loved the most lived, to try and create another home for us that would have love and kindness within it. I wanted them to learn what a real loving home and relationship looked like before they became adults. I could see wounds in them and wanted a chance for them to heal. But my heart was broken over this decision and I suffered greatly being apart from them, even though I lived nearby and shared custody of the children.

Of course few could understand or accept my choice at the time, especially my wife and children. Many of my own family members turned against me. It would be hard to express how lonely and depressed I felt. But I knew I had done this for my children, and for myself, and I still believed my decision was correct. I was committed to at least try the separation out for a time and see what happened.

In dealing with this terrible situation and the suffering all around me, I had few friends or family to talk to. Faced with just myself and my pain, I began to think about who I really was inside in response to my feelings of guilt. There was something inside me that still felt kind and gentle and loving, even though so many people I cared about were angry with me. It took courage and faith to make the choice I made for my children and myself. I gave up so much in the hope that I could create a better life for us, even if I was the only one who believed this. I began to feel so sorry for myself and my children and cried deeply for the pain we all suffered in my hopes of finding something better. This is when my compassion for myself started to flow.

My experience is that the journey to self-love starts with compassion for your own suffering and with the recognition of your own childlike innocence that just wants to be loved. I believe this compassion exists within all of us. But there is a wall of protection over our vulnerable hearts from all the wounds and injustices we have suffered in our lives. The greater the wounds, the bigger the wall. It is difficult to find compassion for anyone when you are filled with pain as this only serves to fortify the wall. We may need to find our way out of pain and into empathy for our own suffering in order to break down the wall around our heart. For me, crying was the right prescription. Just as water can slowly erode even rock, my tears seemed to wear away the wall around my heart.

For those who doubt that love and compassion could exist within themselves, you could think of how you might feel if your own child, parent, sibling or pet was hurt. You need to open your heart to what you care about most deeply and this is where your kindness and compassion can be found. Why shouldn't we be able to feel that for ourselves as well? In the end, no one can tell us exactly where or how to find kindness and compassion for ourselves, as we are all different. But I believe the compassion is there within all of us, and the self-love we need for healing starts with finding this compassion for our own suffering and doubts. If we can feel that for a loved one, it must exist within us, and we are just as deserving of that compassion as anyone.

Once you start feeling compassion for yourself, a subtle shift begins. You can be more gentle with yourself. You begin to understand that you were wounded in your childhood and are doing the best you can. You realize that the way we tend to beat ourselves up makes no more sense than it does to beat up a child because we and the child are one and the same. The mistakes that we all make seem more normal, even human, especially since they are based on fears and self-doubt that arose from the unmet needs we've had since childhood. This behavioral pattern has been passed down by parents to children from generation to generation and no one is to blame.

Then another surprising realization hits you as you begin to look at others with this newfound understanding and compassion. Suddenly you see their suffering in your own suffering and you judge them less, just as you have learned to judge yourself less. You can even see how it is possible to *not* take others judgments against you personally, because their judgments come from their own internal pains. They are not about you. The key to our happiness is how we feel about ourselves, not what someone else thinks about us, and these two things are not necessarily linked together. With this new insight, the possibility of self-love, or even unconditional love of self and others, seems more than a crazy idea. But it all starts with understanding and compassion for ourselves and the basic human condition that we all share.

This brings us back to that old wisdom that you need to love yourself before you can love someone else. I used to think this sounded crazy, like Katlyn did when I first mentioned it to her. My experience was that you needed to look for love and approval from people around you, just as we did as children, so the whole idea of loving myself seemed unrealistic, vain, and self-centered. But once we find compassion for ourselves and see that this allows us to feel compassion for others, the idea of loving yourself first makes perfect sense.

The Master teachers all taught about love. One teaching by Jesus that seems to apply directly to the discussion above is *love your neighbor as yourself.* After learning about the importance of finding inner compassion and self-love first, it seems clear that we could *only* love our neighbor as well as we love ourselves, which may not be that loving at all. This is why, if we are particularly insecure, we struggle with love and tend to avoid relationships or we go through a lot them. I think of this scripture passage now as *love your neighbor as you would want to be loved yourself,* which of course is unconditionally and with complete acceptance as we are. When I fall short of this unconditional love standard, I try to remember that I need to start with myself. And when I encounter a relationship problem, I try not to blame the other person, as this is not helpful. The solution is often within my power if I let go of my expectations of the other person and accept them as they are.

Therefore, I would like to differentiate the word "love" as used in this chapter from "romantic love." Romantic love is a form of conditional love where we initially become infatuated with the other person. When we are needy for love and attention, we can quickly "fall-in-love" with someone we may barely know. Our love inevitably grows out of this phase as our less desirable characteristics become more apparent and we each fail to meet the other person's expectations. Then the underlying dynamic of conditional love takes over, when romantic love can become more of a painful attachment relationship where characteristics of both love and hate may be present. When I speak of love, therefore, romantic love is not what I am referring to. But for some people, this is the only "love" they know, which can make love an emotional word that is not helpful for our discussion.

If this describes you, I suggest that you use the word "kindness" instead, which I think is equivalent to authentic love. You cannot have true kindness without love behind it. We also understand kindness better, as we can see it in a simple smile or gesture. When someone holds a door open for us, stops their car so we can pull ours into a crowded street, or smiles and says thank you when we are only doing our job, we all know this is pure kindness. They are not looking for something in return other than the pleasure of seeing us happy. We should also know that *un*kindness never comes from love, even though some would tell us otherwise. So if the idea of "loving" yourself seems impossible, just try to be more kind and gentle with yourself. Think of how kind and gentle you would be with an injured and crying child. That is what you need.

All religions and belief systems speak of love, both love of God and the love we should have for each other. For Christians, perhaps the most recognizable Bible passage on love is from the Gospel of Mark and it provides Jesus' answer to the question of what is the most important of all God's commandments: *Love the Lord your God with all your heart and with all your soul and with all your mind and with all your strength. The second is this: Love your neighbor as yourself. There is no commandment greater than these.* I noted earlier that Jesus' intention here regarding the love of others might be understood as trying to love others as *we would want to be loved ourselves.* The idea that we may need to learn to love ourselves first in order to best love others or even God is consistent with these commandments.

The Muslim holy book, the Quran, stresses that acts of kindness and compassion are more important than strict observance of rituals: *It is not righteous that you turn your faces to the East or the West, but truly righteous is he who believes in Allah and the Last Day and the angels and the Book and the Prophets, and spends his money for love of Him, on the kindred and the orphans and the needy and the wayfarer, and those who ask for charity,...* (Al Quran 2:178); The emphasis here is both on love of God and love of others, like the Christian scriptures. The Quran also speaks of using good to turn your enemies into friends, *And good and evil are not alike. Repel evil with that which is best. And lo, he between whom and thyself was enmity will become as though he were a warm friend... and none is granted it save those who possess a large share of good* (Al Quran 41:35-36). This is consistent with the Bible verse from the Gospel of Matthew where Jesus tells us to love our enemies *You have heard that it was said, 'Love your neighbor and hate your enemy.' But I tell you, love your enemies and pray for those who persecute you, that you may be children of your Father in heaven.*

The sacred writings of the Hindu faith include the *Bhagavad Gita*, or "Song of the Lord," which contains a dialogue between Krishna, who for Hindus is the embodiment of the God Vishnu on earth (as Jesus embodied God for Christians) and Arjuna, a warrior facing battle. In the text, Krishna calls Arjuna to selfless action in the loving service of God and others, consistent with other faiths. Mahatma Gandhi called the *Bhagavad Gita* his "spiritual dictionary," and his life is widely seen in India as a modern day reflection of its teachings. The *Bhagavad Gita* also states that "We are what we seek" or "Thou art that," which brings us to the Eastern wisdom that all that we seek is within us. This would of course include love and compassion. Buddhism is also quite clear on this point. The Buddha taught that looking outside of ourselves for anything leads to suffering, which is the lesson we learn from our search for love from others.

The Buddha's teachings on loving-kindness (*Metta Sutta*) states, in part: *This is what should be done by those who are skilled in goodness and who know the path of peace: ...Wishing, in gladness and safety, may all beings be at ease... Let none through anger or ill-will wish harm upon another. Even as a mother protects her only child with her life, so with a boundless heart should one cherish all living beings; radiating kindness over the entire world:...* In Buddhism, the metta practice begins with first wishing ourselves loving-kindness in the form of happiness, peace of mind, health of body, and freedom from danger. Then it goes on to make similar wishes for family and friends, those we don't know, and even those who have harmed us. Consistent with the idea that we must learn to love ourselves first, the loving-kindness practice starts with ourselves. The Dalai Lama, spiritual leader of the Tibetan Buddhists, has said, "My religion is very simple. My religion is kindness."

Traditional Chinese religions or philosophy come mainly from Confucius (also known as Master K'ung) through his teachings in the *Analects* and the *Five Classics*, and from Lao Tzu through his teachings in the *Tao Te Ching* and the *Chuang Tzu*. Confucius taught how to live in order to create a moral and harmonious society. His emphasis was on respect for and deference to parents, husbands, and rulers. His ideas still have a large influence on Chinese society today. Confucius' basic moral rule was, *What you do not want done to you, do not do to others.* This is equivalent to the Western golden rule, *do unto others as you would have them do unto you.* Lao Tzu provides similar guidance for living a good life in the *Tao Te Ching* as follows: *See the world as yourself. Have faith in the way things are. Love the world as yourself. Then you can care for all things.* Once again we see the clear emphasis on love and kindness for all, or simply love others as ourselves.

Based on a review of major religions, we can conclude that ancient wisdom teachings agree on the importance of love for everyone, even our enemies. Western religions emphasize that this love comes from God, where Eastern traditions speak of finding the love within ourselves. Since from the Eastern perspective, we are one with the

Universal Spirit, the idea of finding love within ourselves might be seen as finding the love from the God or Holy Spirit within us. They might call this our Buddha nature or inner Brahman. In the end, the differences between religions on this subject of love and where to find it may be more in perspective and less in substance.

In addition to love, many religions teach "fear of God," particularly the Islamic Quran used by Muslims and the Bible's Old Testament, used by both Christians and Jews. According to these faiths, we are told to both love God and fear God, or love God and our neighbor because we fear being sent to hell after death. Eastern religions tell us that love and fear are opposites, as are light and dark, and that love and fear cannot coexist. Even the Gospel of John states: *There is no fear in love, but perfect love casts out fear,* so there appears to be conflicting direction for Christians. I felt both love for and fear of my father growing up, as he had a bit of a temper, so I did not want to upset him. But most of us would agree that it would be difficult to hold feelings of love and fear inside simultaneously because it's hard to feel love if you don't feel safe. And too much fear, especially between a child and parent, can lead to anxiety and depression. So is fear of God and each other really what we want?

If we question what purpose fear serves, we may find a potential solution to this conflict. When disciplining a child, I acknowledged earlier that use of fear could be effective, but there may be better alternatives. The model of loving parental discipline I proposed was based on showing our child that certain behaviors have negative consequences for them and others, but at the same time assuring them they are loved. Our children are better off learning to think about the consequences of their actions for everyone, rather than learning to fear punishment. This helps them learn to make the most loving choice, instead of basing their choices on fear. After all, fear and anxiety is our problem. It keeps us from happiness and well-being and in the worst cases, it effects our physical heath and leads to emotional dysfunction and violence.

In terms of whether or not we need to fear God, perhaps the Eastern religions have an understanding that may be helpful. They believe in Karma, which teaches that our actions have consequences both here and in the afterlife, just like Western religions. They do not teach fear, however, as they know of its negative effects. So perhaps the God of Western religions does not wish us to live in fear of Him, but only to understand the consequences of our actions so we can make better choices, just as we would want for our children. In that way, our fears would not get in the way of giving and receiving the love that He wants for us, or even for our enemies.

It is understandable that humans would use fear as a primary approach to motivating behavior, as that is where our survival instincts lead us. If we were not good at feeling and reacting to fear, we would not have survived as a species. Even our recent human history shows us a world dominated by force and fear. This is what we have known for all of time. It is not surprising, therefore, that some ancient scriptures would tell us to fear God, even if that may not be what the Master teacher intended. Remember, the Master did not write the scriptures. They were passed along verbally and written down much later. No matter what you believe about fear, evidence shows there is a more positive basis for human relationships if we want to be happy and prosper in the complex and interdependent world we live in today. It depends on love and kindness, for ourselves and others, and finding that depends on letting go of some fears.

An interesting discussion of what modern science has learned about our need for love comes from Jonathan Haidt in his book *The Happiness Hypothesis*. Haidt is currently a Professor of Ethical Leadership at New York University's Stern School of Business. His book traces the evolution in modern science's understanding of the child-parent relationship and its impact on our development and well-being as adults. Earlier theories on child development had postulated that children learned best from conditional rewards and punishment used to reinforce or discourage certain behaviors. Unconditional love and acceptance was thought to weaken children and make them spoiled or lazy.

This all changed in the 1950's with research conducted by Harry Harlow at the University of Wisconsin on a colony of rhesus monkeys that he and his students had bred in captivity. His experiments with baby monkeys demonstrated conclusively that babies need physical contact with a mother (or a surrogate) in order to develop as normal, healthy adult monkeys. Similar research on human development later showed that children need parental touch and love just as importantly. The parental love and connection we receive or don't receive critically impacts our childhood development and our future adult relationships.

John Bowlby, an Englishman who knew and supported Harlow, put forth a framework for understanding this parent-child relationship called *Attachment Theory*. Haidt provides the following comment from Bowlby: *When children are separated from their attachment figures (normally parents) for a long time, as in a hospital stay, they quickly descend into passivity and despair. When they are denied a stable and enduring attachment relationship, they are likely to be damaged for life.* Bowlby's research showed that about one-third of American children had an insecure attachment relationship with their parent and would either suppress their distress and try to manage it on their own or would become extremely upset when separated from their parent.

Behavioral psychologists later determined that the patterns we developed in parent-child relationships were repeated as adults. In other words our security or insecurity with our parental relationships determined how we thought about and behaved within our adult relationships. Secure and positive parental relationships normally led to the same as adults, with the reverse being true as well. My lack of parental love and attention was surely a factor in making me insecure and needy in my early adult relationships. Most of us, no matter what type of parenting we received, have still experienced the stress of being separated from people we love, even when that separation is just emotional, like during an argument. And many of us have reacted by suppressing our distress or becoming extremely upset like the insecure child.

Modern science tells us that we need strong and stable loving relationships to be happy and healthy, not only as children but also as adults. Haidt points out that this fact would seem to contradict Eastern wisdom teachings on non-attachment, as the child needs a stable attachment to a parent for survival and proper development, and we carry that need into adulthood. But we also know that adult relationships can be built on unhealthy attachments, as abusive relationships often are, and that we need to learn to love ourselves first before we can truly love others. So how should we think about this childhood need for attachment that we carry into adulthood?

Perhaps the ideal adult relationship is based on a shared "loving connection," and not on attachment. This loving connection would be different than the attachment of a child as we would not depend upon others for survival or to establish our self-worth. If we learn to love ourselves first and build sufficient self-esteem, then we could approach our relationships less from the neediness of a child, and more as an expression of our own loving nature and our desire to serve both ourselves and others.

Chapter Summary

Finding love and kindness, first for yourself and then all others, is the most important principle to live by that I would propose. If you have suffered for lack of love as a child, as so many of us have, learning to love yourself may require substantial time and effort for healing your emotional wounds. But there is nothing that could impact your happiness and well-being more.

Every single Master teacher taught us to love. All scientific evidence shows that after we fulfill our basic survival and security needs, there is nothing more fundamental to human well-being than love and connection to others. Our deep personal longing for love and acceptance tells us this is true. But looking outside ourselves for love can lead us to pain and suffering, as we fail to meet the expectations of others and they fail to meet ours. So it all starts with *learning to love ourselves a lot more,...and then everything else will fall into place,* as Katlyn said.

In my experience, learning to love myself began with first finding compassion for my own suffering and recognizing my own child-like innocence. This was just the start of a long journey that I am still on. There is a saying that I learned while working in China that seems to apply here; *It may sound simple, but it is never easy.* The not-so-easy path to finding self-love and healing is where we go next.

Chapter 3

Acceptance

Serenity now!

—Frank Costanza

If you watched the TV sitcom *Seinfeld*, it is hard to forget the episode when George Costanza's father Frank would shout *Serenity now!* every time he became overly stressed. He wanted to reduce his blood pressure and needed a reminder to bring him some peace of mind when things got too stressful. Shouting this mantra was Frank's approach. If you have never seen this, you could get a good laugh watching the *Best of serenity now* at www.youtube.com. You would see that the shouting worked against Frank as it seemed to only increase his anxiety. Taking a couple of slow, deep breaths would have worked much better. The trouble is, peacefully accepting things as they are goes completely against our human nature and culture.

First, our survival instincts tell us that as soon as we get comfortable with the way things are, we're dead, literally. Can you imagine what happened to a peaceful cave man? Right, there was no such thing, at least not for long. He became dinosaur lunch.

Those genes were not passed down. Our early survival depended on aggressively interacting with our environment to get what we needed and defend ourselves against attack. There was nothing peaceful or accepting about our evolutionary path.

Next, in the modern world we face a ubiquitous business and advertising culture whose own survival depends on us *not* accepting the way things are, but instead becoming highly motivated to look better, have more and nicer stuff, experience amazing places, and be constantly entertained. The list goes on and on. Their worst nightmare is that we become comfortable with the way things are and stop wanting what they are selling. They have more than enough money to constantly influence us to ensure that we don't become comfortable. Pretty much everywhere we look we see their unspoken message, *If you just had this, you'd be happier.* Good luck with acceptance in our society.

Lastly, as discussed in the previous chapter, we grow up insecure from conditional love and acceptance at home and at school. We learn that the best way to gain the approval of others is to conform to their expectations and we either meet them or suffer their rejection. This does not help us learn acceptance, particularly of ourselves. Additionally, in our crowded world we frequently encounter people who are self-absorbed and inconsiderate. Bad stuff seems to happen to us all the time. There appears to be little opportunity for peaceful acceptance in our daily living. This was Frank Costanza's problem. With the deck stacked so high against us, both genetically and culturally, why would we even entertain the idea of acceptance?

Perhaps because there is one simple truth that we cannot escape. Very little of this world is within our control. We cannot control others and at best we can control just some of our own thoughts and actions. I say only some, because our genes and conditioning control a great deal of our thoughts and actions. Thus, control of even ourselves is limited. We'll talk more about that later. For now, just know that we control very little of anything, and with that in mind, learning to accept what we cannot control only makes sense, otherwise we drive ourselves crazy.

The popular Serenity Prayer, which was published by American theologian Reinhold Niebuhr in 1951, has some sage advice on this topic. The most famous lines are the first six:

God, give me grace to accept with serenity
the things that cannot be changed,
Courage to change the things
which should be changed,
and the Wisdom to distinguish
the one from the other.

Let's dissect this prayer for a moment. First, we should accept *the things that cannot be changed.* This would include the things we have no control over, like other people. That may seem obvious, but I would submit, is not easy. It is natural to try to manipulate and control others to get what we want, but this is a losing cause. Next, we change the things *which should be changed.* That sentence is more troublesome, as who defines what things "should be changed"? If we let ourselves run wild with that notion we can end up back where we started, wanting to change everything about ourselves and our world. This does not sound like serenity to me. So what "should be changed" is a dangerous concept that we will need to explore. It does take *wisdom* to distinguish between what cannot be changed and what should be changed.

The obvious point is this: if we set out to change things that cannot be changed or should not be changed, we waste our limited energy and we frustrate ourselves. This is not a recipe for happiness. I am not suggesting that we should ignore or deny that our life and the world we experience is less than it could or should be. Seeing life critically is part of our nature. The difference with acceptance is in developing the understanding to know what cannot or should not be changed and the mental discipline to let these things go and not dwell on them. Discernment, patience, and tolerance are the virtues we need to develop.

As with love and kindness, acceptance starts with the self. It is not possible to accept others when we harshly judge ourselves. When we don't receive the love we need, we believe there must be something wrong with us. This is often what we are told. If everyone loved and accepted us the way we are, this self-judgment would not occur. It is learned from our environment. When we have suffered long enough trying to gain love and acceptance from others, we hopefully find some compassion for ourselves and begin the process of looking inside. If we allow ourselves to go deep enough, most of us will encounter a wounded child.

In this place of pain and compassion, how do we come to understand what cannot or should not be changed about ourselves? Put differently, how do we come to greater self-acceptance?

We need to start with our thoughts and feelings. Common sense would tell us that we first need to explore what we think and feel about our experiences, as this is where we construct our self-image. Professional therapists will tell you the same. But we resist self-exploration because we are ashamed of our thoughts and feelings and need to protect our fragile self-esteem. Katlyn said she hated therapy because it was too painful. So we first need to recognize our suffering and believe that help may be possible, and then we have to ask for help or commit to a practice to get in touch with our internal thoughts and feelings. More simply, we must want help and have the courage to seek it out. The helpful practices that I have experienced are professional therapy, journaling, meditation, and prayer.

Perhaps the most common type of professional therapy is called cognitive therapy, which was invented by Aaron Beck, a psychiatrist at the University of Pennsylvania. His book, *Cognitive Therapy and the Emotional Disorders*, describes this approach. He observes that our emotional problems come from distorted views of reality based on incorrect premises or assumptions we acquire during our development. Such distorted views normally arise because we do not receive the love and acceptance that we need as a child. He provides a relatively simple formula for treatment: *The therapist helps a patient to unravel his distortions in thinking and to learn alternative, more realistic ways to formulate his experiences.* The therapist helps the patient explore their thoughts and feelings in order to identify and correct the misconceptions that are causing sadness, depression, and anxiety. Here the focus is not on changing the world around us, but on changing how we think and feel about it. This is in perfect harmony with the Serenity Prayer—accepting the things that cannot be changed; changing the things that should be changed.

According to Beck, the thoughts and feelings at the source of our emotional suffering are often exactly the type we have been discussing. They arise from the failure and rejection we have experienced throughout our lives. We think, *I am not good enough.* In more serious cases we tell ourselves, *Nothing ever goes right for me.* In the worst cases, we decide, *My life is hopeless.* Beck points out that such thoughts are most often automatic, meaning we are not consciously aware of them. But with a therapist's help, we can catch this negative self-talk that immediately proceeds our stressful moments and then find more accurate and constructive ways of thinking. We can learn that our wounded child is not to blame for the lack of love we have experienced. From this more realistic and positive view of ourselves within the context of our experiences, the idea of greater self-acceptance becomes possible.

Another type of practice that can be very helpful is journaling. With a journal, we make an effort to write down our observations, thoughts, and feelings in the present moment. Because the journal is private, we are not threatened by what others may think of us and we do not have to shape our thoughts to please others, such as we might do with a therapist or friend. The process of writing slows down our mind and allows time to reflect and consider what goes on inside us. Over time, through review and introspection, we can gain insight into the causes of our unpleasant feelings and recognize potential solutions. The missing element is someone to support our process and help suggest alternative ideas or solutions. A self-help or spiritual book could provide some practical advice in this regard, but most of us need a good friend, family member, or therapist to talk to in order to get the greatest benefit from our journaling. Still, the journal is best kept private so we can be honest with ourselves about our thoughts and feelings.

Meditation is a practice that originated in the East, but is now common worldwide. It is a method of mind training that has been shown to reduce anxiety, improve health, and increase focus and memory. There are many types of meditation practices, but what most have in common is sitting comfortably, focusing attention on the breath, gently observing thoughts that arise, then trying to let thoughts go without judgment and returning attention to the breath. This is difficult at first, but the beginner is encouraged to repeatedly start again, returning attention to the breath without judgment, thereby learning patience and self-acceptance. Eventually we start to identify our automatic thought processes, much like cognitive therapy, and we are better able to choose our thoughts and actions instead of reacting based on genetic biases or conditioning.

Dan Harris, the ABC News correspondent, wrote an entertaining book called *10% Happier* about his experiences with a demanding TV news career, the resulting anxiety this caused, and the benefits he received from a meditation practice. He was initially a meditation skeptic, but overcame his doubts in part because of the abundance of scientific evidence supporting its benefits. Harris notes that Harvard University researchers conducted magnetic resonance imaging (MRI) scans on the brains of a large number of people who had been through a standard eight-week meditation course called Mindfulness Based Stress Reduction. The results showed brain growth in areas associated with awareness and compassion, while the regions associated with reaction to stress actually shrank. That is, meditation literally changes the physiology of our brains. This supports Harris' experience that meditation helps one learn to respond to situations more thoughtfully, instead of reacting emotionally.

Prayer is personal, varied, and often specific to a religious practice. Despite this variability, scientific studies show the benefits of prayer are similar to meditation. Many people overlap the two practices by using a prayer or mantra during meditation. People who pray are healthier, happier, and have better focus and concentration. My mother taught us to pray daily, and we did so as a family before bedtime. She also prayed quietly throughout her day. Her faith in God was the bedrock foundation of her life of love and service. In a real sense, she always had someone to share her anxiety with and ask for help. I remember her once telling me when I asked her to pray for my business, which was struggling at the time, that *God always answers our prayers, but sometimes the answer is no.* Still, she believed that she was given everything she needed from God and that by her faithful actions she was earning a place with Him in heaven. That belief made the challenges of her life much easier to accept with grace.

Thus, acceptance is a key principle to live by as it's the only path to peace of mind. Even though we see people and things all around us that we wish were different, since they are out of our control, we need to let them go or we become frustrated and angry. When we constantly judge ourselves, it is not possible to accept others, so acceptance must start with ourselves. This why Katlyn said, *I need to love myself a lot more.* I have discussed some basic practices —therapy, journaling, meditation, and prayer—that have been helpful for me in gaining a better understanding of myself and moving toward self-acceptance. We'll talk more about a daily practice in Chapter 7.

Next I share some of my related experience with healing and acceptance within my first marriage. I offer my experience only as an example that you may be able to relate to your own life experience to gain greater understanding. My memory is imperfect, like all humans, and is limited to only my perspective on what occurred. So please accept my limitations and try not to read judgment or blame into my personal story, as none is intended.

As mentioned in the previous chapter, due to my unmet need for love and attention as a child, I was pretty desperate to find a loving relationship in my teens. I had started dating my future wife our senior year in high school, fell deeply in love with her, and believed she felt the same about me. We went to different colleges, but openly spoke of getting married after we graduated. Things changed our freshmen year. She began dating a popular senior at her college and did not tell me. That is, she secretly dated us both at the same time. I found out about nine months later when her mother jokingly mentioned to me that she didn't know which boyfriend was coming over to the house, as though I knew there was another one. This was a complete shock and it devastated me, as in my mind, she was "the one." My heart was badly broken and I became quite depressed. It took her some time to end her relationship with the other man and she could never explain to me what went wrong with us or why she needed another boyfriend.

We saw each other off and on for the rest of our college years, not dating each other seriously, but never letting go of our relationship either. Near the end of my senior year in college I came to believe once again that she was the person I was meant to spend my life with. Since I was moving away to take a new job and was afraid to lose her, I asked her to marry me. She said yes, but in a less than ecstatic way. Her lack of excitement at the time concerned me, but the wedding planning seemed to go well and I was very hopeful about our future. On our wedding day one year later, I could see something was wrong. She looked terribly uncomfortable and it was more than just nerves. Her mind was clearly somewhere else and this pattern continued into our first year of marriage.

After the wedding, we moved about three hours away where I had been living and working. I tried everything I knew to make her happy and suffered from her lack of affection for me. About six months into our marriage, when I finally pleaded with her to tell me what was wrong, she confessed that she was not ready to be married, but instead was in love with another man. This was a huge surprise and shock to me, similar to how I felt when it happened our freshmen year in college. The man she loved was a former college professor whose name I had only heard mentioned a few times in passing. I asked why she agreed to marry me if she was in love with him, and she said because she was afraid of losing me (not because she loved me).

This was an extremely rough way to start our marriage and a serious blow to my already fragile self-esteem. Once again, I was not enough for her and did not understand why. I couldn't help feeling like an idiot for letting this happen to me again, only now with us married the stakes were much higher. She gave no reasons and I was too ashamed to tell anyone, so I kept it inside and again became very depressed. Divorce was not an option because of my religious beliefs. Plus, I still loved her and believed that in time she might come to love me again. I was deeply hurt and angry with her, but also not one to give up easily. In the end, I decided to accept my situation, take a passive approach, not fight with her over it, and do my best to be a good husband. And I prayed that we would somehow find our way back to the loving and happy relationship we had when we first started dating.

In the hope of bringing us closer together I wanted to have a child. We had always spoken of having children and I naively thought a baby could be just what we needed to bring love into our home. I made the decision to have unprotected sex without discussing it with her first and she became pregnant. While we were blessed with the most beautiful son about two years into our marriage, he was quite a handful as previously mentioned. My wife later expressed anger at me for getting her pregnant without her agreement and said she was not ready to be a mother. In hindsight, this was a fair statement because with our fragile relationship neither of us was really ready to be a parent. So despite the wonder of our newborn son, instead of bringing us closer, our child became another source of stress between us and pulled us further apart.

And so our marriage and family began. We both worked to make the best of things and to be good parents, but there was a serious lack of trust between us. We should have entered couples counseling. However, I had no knowledge of therapy at the time and didn't consider this. We had two more beautiful children, another son about three years later, and Katlyn four years after that. Our children became the main focus of my life. It was so easy to give and receive love and affection with them. This was very healing for me as we cuddled, laughed, and played incessantly. We shared the closest thing to unconditional love that I had ever experienced and the very thing I had longed for since my childhood. This is where I started to grow in self-love and acceptance because it's hard to feel bad about yourself when your children love you so much. I remember thinking that their love for us, and us for them, may end up saving our marriage.

We encountered the normal challenges in disciplining our children, but having grown up with twelve brothers and sisters, this was no big issue for me. It was very different for their mom. She had one sister, ten years older, and grew up in a well-kept house with strict rules. My upbringing was the complete opposite. We viewed raising children through our very different experiences and when the boys would inevitably act out or fight, what I would see as normal, she understandably perceived as a problem. This became another source of stress and conflict between us as she wanted me to discipline our children much more firmly. Having a different experience growing up and seeing how our strict discipline hurt my first son, as previously mentioned, I did not want to do it. I still regret raising my voice and disciplining my sons as often as I did. But this was done primarily to satisfy their mom, and even so, it was never enough for her.

Our different ideas regarding discipline came to a head when our first son was in second grade. His teacher, along with his mom, decided he was acting out too much in school. Their recommendation was to medicate him with Ritalin and have him repeat second grade. This really upset me as he was an intelligent, energetic child who was bored by school. He also acted out to get attention based on the lack of love he felt as a child. I knew this all too well from my own experience. Ritalin, like all the ADHD drugs, has serious side effects. And the available information on retention showed that it never helped, but only branded the child as a failure for life. I explained these facts to his mother and said there was no way I would allow it.

Recent research documented in a *New York Times* article called "Natural Fix for ADHD," by Richard Friedman, shows that overly active people diagnosed with ADHD often have an underlying genetic basis that provides advantages for spontaneous, creative and artistic work. There is literally nothing wrong with them other than not being well suited for the often boring and monotonous environments we put them in. This confirmed what I already knew from experience, as my son was always extremely creative and easily bored. We never medicated or retained him in school, and he went on to do well in third grade and at every level of school afterward. He was blessed to have the most loving and accepting teacher in 3rd and 4th grades who seemed to bring out the best in my son and help restore his self-esteem.

As our children grew, my wife became more unhappy. Over time we had been drifting apart due to our strained relationship with each other and our different relationships with the children. Neither of us had the necessary self-esteem or relationship skills to help the other and we were still not considering counseling, which in hindsight was a mistake. She would disagree and argue with me over the smallest things, so I spent a lot of energy trying to avoid confrontations. She regularly told me that I didn't talk to her enough and she also spent a good deal of time talking on the phone. She was not happy staying home but did not want to go back to work. I had come to believe I could not make her happy, so I focused my energy on our children and my work. I tried to get along, but she kept after me to change and this led to arguments. I told her it was hard for me to feel closer when she was so often upset and telling me it was my fault. After nearly twenty years together, I had grown enough in self-acceptance to reject the idea that I was the only problem in our marriage. I realized that her happiness was not in my control. As the Serenity Prayer would say, I was learning to accept that some things *cannot be changed.*

Despite our marital struggles, I still believed it was better for my children that we stay together. That changed with a series of events that made me question this belief. Because I grew tired of arguments, especially in front of the children, I decided that if we were going to stay together our fighting had to stop. When she would criticize me, I would calmly tell her that I understood how she felt, but didn't agree and didn't want to argue anymore. I asked her to get counseling to help with her depression. Further, I asserted that the children did not need more yelling and firmer discipline. They needed more love and understanding. My decision to no longer argue with her and to ask her to get professional help was the last straw. She was infuriated by this and accused me of "always having to be right." I didn't see it that way, as I was not trying to convince her that I was right. I just believed I was doing the best I could and repeatedly arguing over the same things could only cause more harm. I concluded the one thing *that should change* was my willingness to be drawn into a fight.

Soon after my decision to stop arguing, she attempted suicide early one morning by running the car in the garage with the doors closed. I found her in the car in her pajamas as I entered the garage to go to work. This shook me as I could not understand how she could do such a thing with so little provocation and our three children still sleeping in their beds. I wondered if I had inadvertently driven her to it, but also realized I had not even spoken with her that morning. I sought out a therapist for advice and he told me that since she knew I would find her before any harm could be done, this was not a real suicide attempt, but a form of manipulation. I didn't know if this was true, but either way, he thought it was critical that she get help as soon as possible. I relayed his thoughts and again asked her to seek help. But she still refused any form of therapy, maintaining that her only problem was with my behavior. This episode was a shock to an already failing marriage. I didn't tell anyone but my best friend and the therapist as I was still hoping she would get help for the sake of the children and didn't want to make things worse.

Her suicide attempt forced me to reconsider my belief that we were better off together. The day I became convinced that we needed to try something new was when one of my sons came to her defense as I responded to her criticism. He said things to me that I could not believe were coming from his mouth. The words sounded like they came directly out of hers. That moment showed me that my children were beginning to see me through her increasingly angry eyes and not based on the way I treated them. I could not accept that my relationships with my children were being poisoned by her views, or that they would think our marriage was how adult relationships were supposed to be. So I made the decision that day that I needed to try a separation, both for my children and for me.

As noted in the previous chapter, my separation from my family was the point where I hit bottom and had to face my feelings of unworthiness and guilt. I was partly responsible for our problems. I chose this marriage and I chose to have children, even when things between us were very strained. I knew I was needy and didn't have the energy or skills to help her. I could barely keep my own head above water. My children were suffering. Much of my family and friends could not understand or accept my choice, as I never shared my marital problems with them. I was mostly alone and my life-long desire to create a good marriage, loving family, and peaceful home had officially blown up. I felt like a complete failure and cried so hard for my broken heart and those of my children after I left home.

In the hope of finding relief for my suffering, I met with a therapist, began journaling, and started reading self-help books that spoke of love and healing. These efforts collectively helped me begin to recognize the deep insecurity within me from my unmet longing for love and acceptance. I began to understand why I needed to learn to love and accept myself first. It was clear that I had made mistakes in rushing to get married and have children, all because I was desperate for the love of others. My wife's need for love and attention was something I could never satisfy. We both suffered for want of love. In the middle of this sad situation that we had jointly created were my sweet, beautiful children, longing for the same love and acceptance we were missing. I shed many tears over this and had my doubts about whether the separation was the right thing.

These realizations did not by themselves bring about healing. There is a big difference between intellectual understanding and emotional healing. My new understanding just helped me to develop compassion for myself and see the source of my suffering. Emotional healing is still a long process that requires deeper self-examination and the love and support of others. I was quite wounded from the lack of love in my marriage and all those years facing her anger and criticism. I had built an elaborate defense around my heart in order to keep functioning and barely recognized the extent of my emotional wounds. I still needed to get in touch with my deepest thoughts and feelings, a process that had only just begun. I'll explore this further in the next chapter.

Forgiveness is a process by which we let go of negative feelings toward someone who has hurt us. It implies they are the offender and we are the victim. When we are in pain and feeling like someone hurt us, we want them to say, "I'm sorry and I'll never do that again." We try to "accept" their apology and not to hold it against them. Forgiveness seems like the only way to continue a relationship without holding on to anger and blame. This pattern of thinking always starts with the assumption that someone else is guilty of a transgression against us. We blame them and want them to acknowledge and correct their mistake. But persistent blaming is harmful for any relationship.

My wife and I both blamed the other for our marital problems. She regularly brought up mistakes I had made years earlier and used them against me. Despite my apologies and requests for her forgiveness, she would not let them go. This made it increasingly difficult for us to work through even simple disagreements. By comparison, I cannot recall one time when she said she was sorry, not even for marrying me when she was in love with another man. While I realized I was far from perfect, I could not accept that every problem was my fault and eventually blamed her for our struggles. Over time, we each had built up so many wounds and so much anger and blame toward the other that giving and receiving forgiveness seemed impossible.

Acceptance presents a different option. If we see that the mistakes we make are due to our human nature and our internal suffering from mistakes visited upon us, then we are in some ways blameless. It's not that we don't have choices or free will. But our will is not as free as we think. And it is human to make mistakes and learn from them. We can accept that part of our human nature is to be self-centered. Part of being human is to be desperate for love. Part of being human is to feel anxiety and react emotionally. When we see this in ourselves, it is possible to accept that all humans make mistakes. We can learn from our mistakes without drowning in our guilt. We can also learn not to take the mistakes of others personally because they are as human as we are. From this perspective, forgiveness becomes unnecessary.

After my separation, I started by trying to forgive myself and my wife for the mistakes we made and the suffering we put our children through. Over time, I have found it better to let go of guilt and blame, first for myself and then others. I try to find acceptance now, not forgiveness, because I don't expect myself or anyone else to be perfect and don't want to be finding myself or anyone else guilty. Although I will still ask a person to change their behavior toward me if warranted, I no longer need to have an apology. Those who are most insecure are least able to acknowledge their mistakes and offer one. In many cases, we are just doing the best we can. As the poet Maya Angelou says, *When we know better, we do better.*

We should still accept responsibility for our mistakes and try to correct them. In some cases, we may need to make amends. Saying we are sorry to others may also help them let go of their pain and show that we are trying to change our behavior. But guilt and blame are not helpful emotions, and they are at the root of our need for forgiveness. I recommend that we try to view mistakes as part of our human nature, that we try not to blame ourselves or others, and that we consider acceptance instead of forgiveness. It's a more compassionate approach. There is a popular line from the movie *Love Story* that goes, *Love is never having to say you're sorry.* When you are in the presence of unconditional love and acceptance, I believe this is true.

Judgment is related to blame, as in when we judge others. We all do it. It's so easy to find fault with others and criticize. We judge that someone is less than they should be with the implicit thought that we are better than they are. In truth, when we judge someone else we are projecting our own self-judgments onto them. That is, we have established an internal rulebook for our own behavior that we use to judge ourselves. We use that same rulebook to judge others, even though we have no right to apply our standards to their lives. This is projection. Judging others is the opposite of acceptance and it hurts us because it keeps us from connecting to others with love and kindness. If you accept yourself as being human and try not to find yourself guilty, but instead just mistaken, you can accept others the same way and there is no need for judgment. Instead, we can see our unskillful behaviors and those of others with compassion and understanding.

The other problem with projecting our standards for behavior onto another person is that our life experiences are completely different. We can't begin to understand what another person feels inside, even those closest to us, let alone the strangers we encounter and judge every day. The saying that one should not judge until you have *walked a mile in someone else's shoes* is a wise reminder that we all have a unique genetic makeup along with different life experiences and conditioning. A related saying that is equally wise is, *There but for the grace of God go I.* The wisdom here is that if we were born under different circumstances and had the identical physical make up and life experiences as the person we are judging, even the worst criminal, we may have behaved in exactly the same way. Upon reflection, I think we all know this is true. My mother frequently offered us this pearl of wisdom when we would criticize others, *If you don't have something good to say, don't say anything.*

Are we not right to expect certain minimal behaviors from others such as kindness, respect and honesty? Of course we all want these things. But as mentioned earlier, our expectations of others and their expectations of us lead to suffering because we cannot always live up to them. Even when someone is unkind, disrespectful or dishonest, the best approach is to not take it personally or respond in kind. I'm not saying this is easy, just that it is best. We can always ask to be treated respectfully. However, if we return their unkindness or disrespect to them, this leads to escalation and more pain for everyone. Other people do things that hurt us only because they are hurting inside. If they felt kindness, self-respect and honesty inside, they would readily offer that to us.

There is also a difference between judging others and discernment. We correctly have standards for our own behavior and need to assess the world around us to determine what is helpful for us and what is not. This includes people. With discernment, we seek to understand and choose thoughts and actions that are positive for us and avoid those that are negative. This does not require us to find fault with others who make choices that we would not make. We can decide not to engage in an activity with a person, for example, without judging them negatively. We can make the choice that best suits us and still accept them as they are. We can offer them kindness and acceptance from our heart instead of criticism. It's a subtle but important difference that is based on choosing compassion. This choice recognizes that at times we all need to make mistakes in order to learn. The Serenity Prayer would tell us not to try and change others, as they are *things we cannot change.* We should respect others right to choose for themselves, just as we would want the same, so long as their choices are not directly harmful to us.

As with love and kindness, the ancient wisdom teachings regarding non-judgment and acceptance are one-sided. We can start with the biblical wisdom from the Gospel of Luke that we call the Golden Rule. In it Jesus states, *Do unto others as you would have them do unto you.* Confucius taught a version of the same truth, *What you do not want done to you, do not do to others.* It is clear that none of us wants to be judged. We all have reasons for the actions we take. Even when we become fearful or emotionally distressed and act in ways that we may later regret, we are often crying out for help and still don't want to be judged harshly. We prefer compassion and understanding when we make mistakes. This is not normally what we receive and it is difficult for us to offer this to others when we have not yet learned to give it to ourselves.

In the Gospel of Luke, Jesus states more strongly, *Do not judge others, and you will not be judged. Do not condemn others, or it will all come back against you. Forgive others, and you will be forgiven.* In the Gospel of John, Jesus states, *He who is without sin among you, let him be the first to throw a stone at her.* With this clear admonition against judging others directly from Jesus, Christians should be among the least judgmental and most forgiving of all people. Unfortunately, we sometimes forget about Jesus' core teachings on non-judgment and forgiveness and instead apply our standards for faith and behavior to others. We want to be righteous, that is, think and act in accordance with Jesus teachings. But it's another matter to judge those who don't share our beliefs as wrong or evil. There is never a problem with having a moral code and doing what we believe is right, so long it does not harm others. Finding others wrong is the problem, especially if we wish to follow Jesus' teaching to not judge others.

I discussed homosexuality with my loving mother a few years back. She had always taught us not to judge others, but she seemed to feel differently about homosexuality. I asked her how she could reconcile her views of gays, and those of the Catholic Church, with Jesus' teachings. She explained that she did not judge gay people, she only judged their behavior. I can see how this made sense to her. She genuinely felt compassion for gays even though she thought their choices were sinful. For her generation, this was an evolved position. Even when another's choice is not moral for us, we can still accept and support them. We can recognize it is not our place to judge others and offer love instead. Pope Francis had this to say on the subject, *If a person is gay and seeks God and has good will, who am I to judge him?* This is what Jesus taught.

Islam teaches that Jesus is a prophet of Allah and therefore Muslims view his teachings as truth, including those on love and non-judgment. Some Muslims however, like extreme members of all faiths, are intolerant of others to the point of violence. Muhammad also taught compassion and non-judgment. The Quran states the following, *For that reason, believers are forgiving, compassionate and tolerant people who, as revealed in the Quran, control their rage and pardon other people.* [Quran, 3:134]. It is important, therefore, not to judge any religion or its adherents with a broad brush based on the behavior of an extremist minority. There are many places in the world where people of all faiths live in mutual respect and peace. There are also places in the world today where Christians, Hindus, and Buddhists kill others because they have different beliefs. No doubt religious intolerance and the resulting violence is a major problem among some Muslims. This points to a need for greater understanding of the loving and tolerant teachings of Islam and a need for healing of their wounds.

Most of the Eastern religions teach ahimsa, which means to "do no harm" to any living being. The concept includes harm to others by our thoughts, words, or deeds. Since all living beings are considered one with the Divine, harming others serves only to harm ourselves. In addition, the idea of karmic consequences for our actions should lead us away from harming others as this will come back to us. Mahatma Gandhi used ahimsa as a fundamental guiding principle in his life. In his autobiography, *The Story of My Experiments with Truth*, Gandhi speaks of how following the principle of ahimsa led him to non-judgment:

> *Man and his deed are two distinct things. Whereas a good deed should call forth approbation and a wicked deed disapprobation, the doer of the deed, whether good or wicked, always deserves respect or pity as the case may be. 'Hate the sin and not the sinner' is a precept which, though easy enough to understand, is rarely practiced, and that is why the poison of hatred spreads in the world.*

The Buddha gave perhaps the most extensive wisdom teachings on acceptance. His focus was on eliminating suffering by letting go of our attachment to getting what we desire and our aversion to things we judge as undesirable. The alternative to our attachments and aversions is acceptance of life as it is. The word for suffering that the Buddha used, *dukkha*, is broadly understood as dissatisfaction with life and would include the pain, frustration, anxiety, and disappointment that we all experience. The Buddha recognized that our human desires are normal and not by themselves unhealthy. He taught that with meditation, we can begin to see the hold that our desires have on our minds and our happiness. Our suffering is not necessarily based on the circumstances of our life. It is based on how we think about them. Cognitive therapy is founded on the same belief. When our minds obsess over small issues or we grow impatient over the slightest inconvenience, we can see this is true.

The Buddha taught that we should first critically evaluate his ideas on attachment and suffering in our own mind to see if they made intellectual and common sense. If so, we should next seek "direct experience" of the truth of suffering through mindful awareness of our experiences. The way to develop mindful awareness is through meditation practice, where we can become conscious of our internal thoughts and feelings. This leads us to insight and eventually a state where we "know" the truth of suffering. Once we know this, we see that our efforts to control what is inherently uncontrollable are the cause of our unhappiness. For a Buddhist, the key to happiness is acceptance of ourselves and our life as it is. The *Bhagavad Gita*, the sacred Hindu text, likewise states, *The man who casting off all desires, lives free from attachment... obtains tranquility.*

Chapter Summary

Our instinct is to judge ourselves and everything we encounter as good or bad. Society teaches us to never settle for who we are or what we have. But our happiness and peace of mind depend on us accepting things as they are because little of this world is within our control. If we accept the world as it is, the only thing left to change is ourselves. And the most important thing to change about ourselves is the way we think.

This is a key point where modern science and ancient wisdom agree. We don't need to do a better job living up to society's ideals and the expectations of others. We don't need to convince others to live up to our expectations. We *do* need to let go of judgments against ourselves and our world. Acceptance, or non-attachment as the Buddha would say, is the change we need most and it is entirely within our minds.

Learning acceptance starts with finding compassion for ourselves and exploring our thoughts and feelings to gain insight into the source of our emotional anxiety. Therapy, meditation, journaling, and prayer are useful practices for working toward such insights and learning to change our mind. Through such practices we can find the support and wisdom we need to move toward more acceptance and peace of mind.

In my experience, I did not get the love and attention I needed as a child, so I rushed off to get married even though alarm bells were ringing along with the church bells. And when I didn't get the love I needed from my marriage, I rushed off to have children with the same alarms still ringing. These were clearly my mistakes. While interactions with my wife reinforced the deep fears I had since childhood that I was not good enough and not worthy of love, my loving relationships with my children provided the support I needed to start my healing and move toward self-acceptance.

Once this happened, I could no longer accept responsibility for my wife's happiness. I had done my best to love and help her, but eventually realized her happiness was not in my control. As my family grew, I decided that there was no more sense in repeatedly arguing over the same things. When I came to believe that my family might be better off separated, I had to accept the most difficult decision I could have imagined. I moved out of my home, away from the persons I loved most in the world, in the hope of creating something better for us. Then I began my deeper journey of self-exploration and healing out of compassion for all of our suffering.

My greatest challenge with acceptance was still to come. How could I come to accept the choice Katlyn made to leave this world when I loved her with all my heart and did everything within my power to help her? This is the greatest personal tragedy I could have imagined and the last thing I would have expected. It is no exaggeration to say that I would rather have given my own life. For me, learning to accept Katlyn's choice is like initially learning self-acceptance; it goes against everything I feel inside. Even so, I must continue to work for this as I still have much to live for. So with compassion for our combined suffering, I search for greater understanding.

I finish this chapter with one more tribute to Katlyn, left by a dear friend, to show that I am not the only one who is struggling to accept the loss of one so precious.

Your soul - Beautiful
Your smile - Infectious
Loved - Always
Forgotten - Never
Your light lives on inside me. It radiates through my soul, I carry it everywhere I go. I find peace knowing you will be with me where ever I go. As much as my heart hurts I know you are where you want to be. And all I ever want for you is pure happiness just as you've always wanted for me.

OshKosh

Chapter 4

Understanding

Know thyself.

—Plato

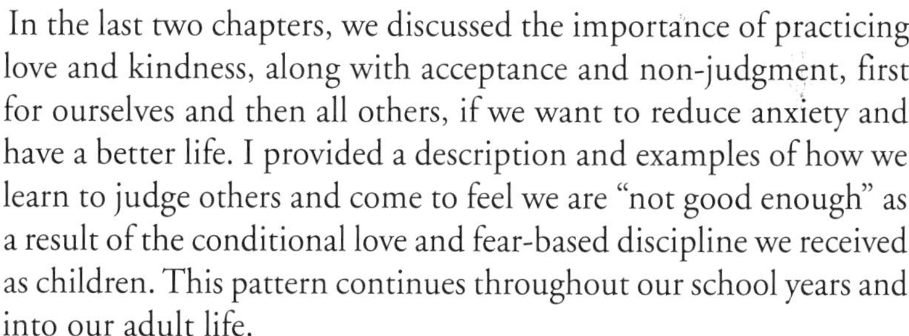

In the last two chapters, we discussed the importance of practicing love and kindness, along with acceptance and non-judgment, first for ourselves and then all others, if we want to reduce anxiety and have a better life. I provided a description and examples of how we learn to judge others and come to feel we are "not good enough" as a result of the conditional love and fear-based discipline we received as children. This pattern continues throughout our school years and into our adult life.

Our genetic makeup and childhood conditioning combine to create negative automatic thoughts in our mind that can lead to anxiety and depression. I covered some practices that help us change our mind by gaining insight into our thoughts and feelings and learning more realistic and constructive ways to think. However, this work of changing our minds is difficult and seems to take forever as we repeat the same negative thoughts and actions over and over. What is it about our mind that makes it so difficult to change? Once we recognize our mistakes, why can't we think and act from our newfound wisdom and understanding instead of continuing to be led by our fears, desires, and emotions?

When it comes to changing our thoughts and behaviors, there are things about our mind and environment that work against us. First, our mind has two distinct parts that are often in conflict. There is the reasoned part of our mind that we understand as our conscious thoughts. This is what you are engaging as you read and consider ideas in this book. Then there is the automatic part of our mind that runs our bodily functions and allows us to drive a car, for example, while we are having a conversation. This is often called our subconscious. The automatic part of our minds contains the subconscious conditioning of our childhood and our human instincts, such as our fight-or-flight reflexes and our desires for food and sex.

Jonathan Haidt, author of *The Happiness Hypothesis,* I previously mentioned, uses an elephant and a rider as a helpful metaphor to illustrate the workings of our divided mind. The elephant, as the metaphor implies, represents the dominant part of our mind, which is the automatic processing and our subconscious. The rider represents our conscious reasoning that seeks to control our thoughts and behaviors. What science has shown, and what we all know from experience, is the elephant has the upper hand. In a head on battle between our reasoned will (rider) and the instinctual and conditioned behavior in our minds (elephant), the elephant usually wins. This is why our fears, desires, and emotions frequently cause us to act in ways we later regret and why we often have difficulty meeting our resolutions.

Haidt believes that while our rider tries to gain control of our mind, it is best seen as an advisor who can only help the elephant make better choices. The "mind changing" practices of therapy and meditation are among those he recommends to train the elephant to think more constructively and long-term. The point in bringing up this metaphor is that we need to understand that in seeking to become more loving and accepting, by changing the negative thought patterns in our mind, we are trying to retrain a very big, and very much automatic and hidden set of processes (the elephant). The rider in our brain can never really control the elephant by willpower alone when its own mind is made up, so what's needed is a sustained retraining effort for the elephant.

Any of us who have trained an animal or pet know this requires a large number of repetitions of desired behaviors with the associated rewards or, in the case of unwanted behaviors, punishments. If the rewards and punishments are not consistently applied with behaviors, then the animal becomes confused and their instincts take over. When we work to retrain our minds through therapy or meditation, for example, we are attempting to do the same. We learn that a certain way of thinking or acting has a more positive outcome (reward) or negative outcome (punishment), and therefore we feel motivated to change. That conscious realization feels promising in the moment. But our problem becomes the consistency of our training, just like with our pet. Unfortunately, one hour per week in therapy, or 30 minutes a day in meditation, for example, is often not enough to overcome the contradictory training we received in our childhood or experience in our daily life.

The examples we encounter daily are usually not kindness and acceptance, but more likely criticism and manipulation. We are told that we are not good enough and taught to judge everything around us. Learning to love and accept ourselves is great in theory, but the majority of our time is spent in an environment that teaches us the opposite. When we and those around us are getting everything we want, there is no problem with love, kindness and acceptance. But this is not the predominant experience for most of us. This is why monks live and train in monasteries, and why churches exist for their followers, or in the case of Buddhism, why a fundamental organizing principle is around the Sangha, or spiritual community.

There is a Native American story about two wolves that seems relevant here:

> One evening an old Cherokee told his grandson about a battle that goes on inside people. He said, *My son, the battle is between two wolves inside us all.*
> *One is Evil – It is anger, envy, jealousy, sorrow, regret, greed, arrogance, self-pity, guilt, resentment, inferiority, lies, false pride, superiority, and ego.*
> *The other is Good – It is joy, peace, love, hope, serenity, humility, kindness, benevolence, empathy, generosity, truth, compassion and faith.*
> The grandson thought about it for a minute and then asked his grandfather: *Which wolf wins?* The old Cherokee simply replied, *The one you feed.*

Our environment provides most of the food for our inner wolves, or elephant, as we have discussed. This can pose a big problem when we seek to change our minds for the better, since environmental influences often run counter to the change we seek, and we have only limited control of our environment. And as though this mind retraining were not hard enough already, there is still one more big obstacle to overcome. Not only is the part of our mind we want to retrain like a huge elephant with a hidden mind of its own, and the training environment we put the elephant into is often inconsistent and counter to what we want to learn, but the elephant's defensive instincts create another huge barrier to this type of retraining. The moment we experience emotional discomfort or any type of personal threat, we run away, go on the defensive, or attack. And this brings us to perhaps the biggest obstacle to retraining our mind. When we feel threatened, which is what being judged or unloved feels like, our automatic defense processes take over.

Our automatic defensive reactions are those that arise from fear, such as *attacking* and *defending*, which are active responses, or *avoidance* and *distraction*, which are passive responses. If you can imagine trying to train a child in positive behaviors, for example, when they are in fear, you can see how this might be a problem. It would be like telling a person under constant threat of physical abuse that they should try to be more kind and considerate. It's hard to learn something positive when you live in fear and are always trying to run away or defend yourself. At this point, the elephant is in survival mode and not listening to the rider. Instead, what we need to heal our negative thoughts and feelings is support and love. In short, we need to feel safe.

What makes this aspect of the elephant particularly difficult to overcome is that our automatic defensive responses are sophisticated. Because of that we're often unaware of being on the defensive. When we angrily react to someone who criticizes us, our defensive response is clear. Less obvious is the way we may withdraw from or avoid any type of conflict to keep the peace, even if we are being mistreated. We may shutdown if our actions are questioned or our thoughts are too painful. Alternatively, we can create a self-story of well-being and fill ourselves with pride and righteousness, also in defense of our insecurities. Fear and insecurity can express itself outwardly in many different ways. What all expressions share in common is they keep us from seeing the pain inside, like we might be forced to look away from a particularly gruesome accident scene. Again, when we feel threatened, automatic self-protection processes take over and the rider has little chance of influencing the elephant.

Our desire to stay constantly busy or distracted can also be a sophisticated defense mechanism. Ask yourself if you have much free time or if you are comfortable being alone without any distraction for hours at a time. I think many of us would say no, or at least say that when we have a choice, we would choose otherwise. When we are wounded and insecure, we don't want to face ourselves and our pain. We run from ourselves and stay as busy as possible. It's a common defense mechanism. This may manifest as constantly being around other people, or working, or watching TV, or surfing the internet, or playing video games, or being on our smart phones. None of these things are harmful by themselves in moderation. But when we are without them and alone, even for a short period of time, and feel anxiety, that's a sign our distractions are keeping us from facing something painful. We normally don't understand the reasons for this, we just know we are uncomfortable when we're not occupied or distracted.

When we obsess over being the best we can be or having more and better material things, this can also be a sophisticated defense mechanism based on insecurity and avoidance. It is normal and healthy to pursue material things along with excellence in all that we do. But we cross the line into obsession when these pursuits become the principal focus of our lives, as they are for many. We can sacrifice our health and happiness, and those of our family and friends, in pursuit of such ends. I asked earlier, when these pursuits go to the extreme what are we trying to prove? My conclusion is that we are likely acting in defense of our insecurities and trying to prove we are worthy. People in this circumstance often remain unaware, because the underlying thoughts behind these behaviors are based on fear and our instinct is to avoid seeing them.

For most of us, our true motivations are more hidden than we realize. When they are based on our fears and insecurities, as they often are, it becomes even more difficult to bring them into the light. We need to feel safe to access this painful part of us. This is one more reason why getting to know our true thoughts and feelings at the source of our anxiety or depression is so difficult. And if we can't get to the truth, we won't be able to resolve these issues and retrain our mind. I will share some of my experiences, and those of Katlyn, encountering these obstacles while trying to retrain my mind to become more loving and accepting.

After my separation, I had serious doubts about my decision because of the emotional suffering I saw from my children, as well as my own in being apart from them. I lived only a few miles away and had shared custody of the children, though they spent most nights with their mother. I wanted to return home badly and considered this option for two years before filing for divorce. When my wife and I discussed getting back together, she was always filled with anger and spoke only of things I needed to change. She never said she loved me or was willing to get help for her depression. We tried couples counseling briefly, but that was not helpful either. I concluded it would likely be worse if I returned. But she did not accept my choice. Instead she went on the offensive.

She recruited my family against me, phoning several of my brothers and sisters and visiting my parents often. I pleaded with her to stop this many times to no avail. My wife also adopted evangelical Christian beliefs at this time, supported by two of my siblings who had joined this type of church. Angry letters from these two siblings soon followed, accusing me of being taken over by Satan and leading a life of sin, all without ever speaking to me. My wife had painted herself as an innocent victim and mentioned none of the problems that had driven us apart for over eighteen years. I could see why some of my family believed her story, as I had never spoken badly about her or told any of them about my marital problems. She had always been so charming around them, acting like the perfect wife and mother, while behaving very differently at home.

I did not try to defend myself or blame her, thinking this would only encourage my family member's involvement and make matters worse. We had learned through couple's counseling to share our marital problems only with a therapist, best friend, or immediate family member, and never, ever to discuss them with our children. The point was to not force family and friends to pick sides and to protect the children from further harm. I feared that if I started telling the truth about her, it would eventually get back to my children and hurt them even more. I wasn't willing to risk harming them further. In response to one of the critical family emails I received at the time, I wrote to a sister:

I am saddened by the rumors and judgments that have come from some of my family. I have debated many times whether I should tell you all the truth of my marriage, believing if you heard my story, you would never blame me. But when I calm down, I see that it would only shift the blame to her, and in fact we are both responsible for this. So I keep choosing what I believe is the higher ground. I went on to say,

She readily admits that our relationship to each other, to the kids, and the kids' relationships to each other have all improved greatly since our separation. She thinks it's a sign that it is time to get back together. I see it as an indication that we are better off apart.

Saying I was saddened was quite an understatement. The angry letters from some family members took a big toll on me. I had left home to escape judgment and negativity and create something better, but now seemed to face even more of it. One benefit of all the criticism I received, however, was that I was completely humbled and forced to let go of my pride. I couldn't understand how things went so wrong in my marriage, or how some of my family did not support me in the same way as I would have supported them, but the situation was still my creation and my responsibility. With little remaining of my hopes and dreams for a loving family and home, I humbly began looking for answers.

I still believed in my inner goodness and loving intentions, so I needed to let go of those people in my life that saw me otherwise. As I learned the limits of love and loyalty within my own family, I began to care less about what other people thought of me. In the end, instead of convincing me to return home, the judgmental actions of my wife and some of my family just convinced me that the love I needed could not be found there.

I kept on reading, praying and journaling, and also began searching for guidance outside my existing circle of family and friends, hoping to find true compassion and understanding for my suffering. I studied books on different religions and philosophies, and met with teachers of different spiritual traditions where I began to see the common elements among them regarding our need for love and acceptance as mentioned in the previous chapters. It was among these new friends and teachers that I found the compassion and understanding I needed to feel safe and begin my path toward emotional healing.

Gaining the deeper self-awareness needed to bring about emotional healing, however, was a long and iterative process for me. Through personal exploration and discussions with counselors, teachers, and friends, I gained insight into my negative thought and behavior patterns, and worked to change them. But eventually my old fears would arise again, often subconsciously, and I would slide back into my old defensive patterns of behavior. Each time I would repeat this process, I had the opportunity to grow a little more, gaining an even deeper understanding of myself, and so hopefully not slide back as far the next time my fear patterns returned. However, I was often surprised reading back over my journal to see how the same problems and issues resurfaced. It seemed I had to learn things over and over again. My process of gaining self-awareness and changing my negative thoughts and actions (that is, retraining my elephant) would require a lot of dedication and persistence to sustain any positive changes.

This "self-awakening" process requires us to keep looking deeper, like peeling back the layers of an onion. My initial insights tended to be more superficial, as it was still too difficult to look at my deepest fears. This is why the initial changes I made were not sustainable, as I often didn't understand the real problem. So coming to a deeper understanding requires the courage to face our deepest pain. But we are so afraid to do this, as though there is a monster lurking in the dark that will kill us if we dare look at it, like the Medusa of Greek legend. But when we turn on the light and look, we realize there is no monster there at all. Instead of the terrible pain we expected to experience, we can find relief. Like many fears, what I had created in my mind was worse than reality. Once I faced my deepest fears, their power over me was greatly diminished.

In time, I saw the pains of my childhood as discussed earlier, and realized that I had been looking desperately for the love and acceptance I missed as a child. As I gained this awareness and found compassion for my own suffering, I learned to listen to my own inner voice because it was more kind and compassionate than that of others. I learned to stop beating myself up because I knew I was doing my best. I eventually learned to offer kindness even to those who had harmed me. With that change, my family relationships healed and I became gentler in all aspects of my life.

Several years later, while on a trail running and meditation retreat in the mountains of Colorado, I received an unexpected affirmation of these positive changes in my life. One of the retreat participants whom I had met just days earlier asked me how I had come to be so kind and peaceful. She said there was a light in my eyes. What was my secret? She said that she and others had initially thought my appearance was contrived, but they had since concluded that it was real and wondered what I had discovered. I was surprised by her questions and remember responding with comments about my personal journey and working hard to become kinder to myself and others. And even though my response felt inadequate at the time, that awkward moment let me know that I had made progress in my quest to outwardly manifest the goodness that I always felt was within me. I believe that same goodness exists within all of us.

As I worked toward self-realization and emotional healing, my children had different experiences with the separation. My boys seemed very hurt and angry with me at first, as one would expect. We normally had fun together at home and I also shielded them somewhat from their mom. But they were older at the time of separation, the oldest sixteen, the second nearing thirteen, and our relationships had a strong foundation. They also spent more time with their friends than at home, so they managed our split with limited outward struggle and seemed to accept it in time. Eventually, each asked me about the divorce to hear my side of the story and I told them two things. I would never have left if I did not believe they would be better off and they saw enough of our marital problems to know the truth. It would only hurt them for me to go into details. They each seemed satisfied with my explanation and hugged and thanked me.

Katlyn had a very different experience. She was just eight at the time of our separation and very much a Daddy's girl. We had all showered her with love and affection since birth and she remained the darling of the family well into her school years. Katlyn was very happy, outwardly self-confident, and engaging. The boys complained that she'd become a little spoiled and was never disciplined, but even her bratty, attention getting moments seemed cute to me. She had no problems with self-esteem as a child, however, this changed when I left home. She took it personally and would not accept my assertion that the separation was between me and her mom and that I still loved her just the same. I told her I was still there for her, just not living in the same house. But she lobbied hard for me to return home and when I didn't she took it very hard.

Over the following years, Katlyn became outwardly depressed and distanced herself from me. I kept trying to show her that I loved her by seeing her as often as possible and taking her on vacations with just the two of us. But eventually she would refuse to sleep over at my house, would be relatively silent when we got together, and often would not return my calls. I could see she was suffering, but she would not talk to me about it. I was unsure how much of this was her still struggling with our separation and divorce, and how much was the normal behavior of a teenage girl.

Our relationship problems thankfully came to a head in June 2007 when she was seventeen years old. She called me after midnight crying on the phone and accused me of being a terrible father and causing her pain. I quickly drove to her house and spent the next couple hours holding her in my arms, listening to her, trying to console her, and assuring her that I wanted to understand everything she was feeling. I took notes and promised her that I would do better. I was just so relieved that she finally had the courage to tell me how she felt. The next morning I wrote this in my journal:

Last night Katlyn called very angry at me and said so many things that I promised to write down so I would never forget. They are: I am a terrible father - I ruined her life when I left home and didn't come back - I have no idea how hard it is for her - I don't even know her - She feels so terrible about herself - She has no friends because she has such low self-esteem - She feels so ugly (wants me to pay for a nose job) - She feels so unworthy and unloved - I never went to see any softball games this year - I don't ever go to her school to meet her teachers - She hates that I don't support her at (her high school) *- I never say anything good about her - I never come to see her anymore now that she has a car - She can never talk to her counselor about me because every time my name comes up, all she can do is cry - Mom still loves me and can't marry* (her boyfriend) *- She is so afraid Grandma is going to die - Grandma is so bad - Tasha* (her dog) *is really blind and bumping into things - The house needs so much work - Grandma is always going to the hospital - Mom can't do anything except look after Grandma -* (Katlyn's boyfriend) *is so angry over his Grandpa's death and snaps at her now - She is so angry that she snaps at friends - All her friends from town have changed so much - They are all so caught up in gossip and being cool - All the kids* (in high school) *are into drinking and smoking pot and having sex - We never talk about anything - She doesn't return my calls because she is mad at me - She loves being with her brothers and me the most - She misses* (her oldest brother) *so much and wishes he would come and stay at the house more - Mom yells at her because that is all she knows how to do when she gets mad - She yells at Mom because that is all she knows how to do - She has been so afraid to tell me how she feels or yell at me because she was afraid to drive me further away - She is so scared that* (her boyfriend) *would leave her - She feels so stupid and has to study so hard in school - She doesn't want me to tell her I love her, she wants me to show her.*

I read my journal notes to Katlyn to make sure she knew that I understood her and was not angry with her at all. It didn't matter that she called me a terrible father, because I knew I had never stopped trying to love her and give her what she needed. All I wanted now was to show her how much I loved her and help relieve her suffering. I had written a commitment in my journal to be a better father, which I also read to Katlyn:

Things I need to be a better father to Katlyn:

1. *Spend more time with her. Don't take no for an answer.*
2. *Go to her house and pick her up. Don't always make her drive to me.*

3. *Spend a lot of time with just the two of us.*
4. *Don't ever joke about her looks,* (high school), (boyfriend), *or almost anything. Her self-esteem is so fragile.*
5. *Tell her how amazing she is as much as possible.*
6. *Tell her how much I appreciate and admire her hard work in school and sports.*
7. *Take her and* (her brother) *out together and go visit her at home together.*
8. *Find a way to settle things with Mom, visit her and help Mom out with the house.*
9. *Think about Katlyn every day and ask what I can do for her.*

While I was grateful for the courage Katlyn showed in finally expressing all her pain, I felt overwhelmed by the number of burdens she was carrying. She expressed anxiety about me, her looks, intelligence, self-esteem, friends, boyfriend, mother, brother, grandma, dog, house, school, peers, and seeing a counselor. My own insecurities from childhood were nothing compared to hers. Added to her own pain, she had taken on the suffering of everyone she cared about. This was very frightening to me, as it was much worse than I had imagined and beyond my ability to really comprehend.

My compassionate response to her emotional outburst caused an immediate shift in our relationship. Katlyn could see by my actions now that I really did love her and realized that she had been pushing me away. She also saw that I was willing to give her what she needed. The compassion and understanding I had gained through my personal journey is something I could now offer to her. She was less afraid to talk to me now and began to ask for advice about her problems and the fighting at home between her and her mom. She told me that her mother had always said, *You left US and didn't love US,* and now that she knew it wasn't true, her anger and fighting with her mother intensified.

I expressed my concerns to her mom over the continued yelling at home and told her there is only one effective way to respond to Katlyn's emotional outbursts of pain and anger. We have to help her feel safe (don't shout back), we have to show her kindness and compassion (listen and let her know you care), and we have to help her find a way to get what she needs (show her there's a solution). This is not easy when we feel angry and threatened ourselves, but the parent needs to offer compassion and understanding or the cycle of suffering will not stop. This is what I did when Katlyn yelled at me and what I wanted for her at home. But her mother disagreed with me as usual and blamed me for not coming down hard enough on Katlyn.

I was also concerned that her mother continued to tell Katlyn she was "in love with me" and couldn't marry her long-time boyfriend, nine years after our separation and three years after I had remarried. I had told Katlyn before that her mother should not put these emotional burdens on her. The idea that she was "in love with me" seemed untruthful, and even if her mother believed this, it was a terrible example of "love" for Katlyn. I also reminded her mother of our joint counseling session for parents of divorce where we were specifically warned against saying bad things about the other parent or discussing our relationship problems with our children.

But her mother's stories that I didn't love *them* anymore, and that she was still in love with me and couldn't remarry, served her purpose in gaining Katlyn's compassion and loyalty by continuing to play the victim, while at the same time blaming me and my new wife for her suffering. Just as she had done with my family when we first separated, her fabrications would punish me by keeping Katlyn away from me. Unfortunately, while this served her mother's needs, it also deeply hurt Katlyn.

The reason I share my own experience after separation, that of my sons, and those of Katlyn and her mom, is that they demonstrate aspects of understanding addressed earlier. For my own healing, the lesson was simple. I needed to feel safe to begin to understand my inner suffering and motivations. Unfortunately, I was not able to find this while in my marriage. This started after I searched for new friends and spiritual teachers and found true compassion and understanding. My instinct in leaving home was correct, as

I became a more peaceful and loving father once I was no longer being attacked. My sons were eventually able to accept my decision because they had been around me long enough to feel confident of my love and feel safe with me. Years later, my oldest son told my parents that they needed to *get over the divorce* because his mother and I were completely different people and therefore much better off apart.

Katlyn, however, did not have either the time with me or the maturity level to feel safe and experience our divorce the same way. Katlyn needed to accept my decision and recognize that I loved her and was there for her, just like the boys. But she was not taught acceptance. Instead she was told that I had abandoned her and no longer loved her. Like her mother, she felt victimized and blamed me for her pain. If her mom had accepted my decision and told Katlyn how much I loved her and that our divorce had nothing to do with her, she would have accepted it sooner and avoided much suffering and depression. But her mom's refusal to accept our separation and divorce became Katlyn's refusal as well. This is why understanding our own fears and insecurities is so important, especially for parents. Otherwise, we can put them on our children to their great detriment.

We should also understand the profound circumstances of raising our voices in anger at a child or anyone else. Shouting is a pure defense mechanism for our insecurity. It is also a type of emotional abuse that is every bit as damaging as physical abuse. It can be equally traumatic as it inflicts deep emotional wounds that are not outwardly visible, but still in desperate need of healing. Both physical and emotional abuse show you that you're not safe and you're not worthy. In addition, when emotional abuse is inflicted on a child, it teaches them the wrong way to handle pain and injustice. The child becomes emotionally dysfunctional when threatened, just like the parent. I have experienced both sides of this and those who knew Katlyn well surely witnessed the emotional side of her.

At least with physical abuse, there are hospitals to get healing, laws to make it stop, and support groups to help you when you've endured it. However, you could be emotionally abused for your entire life and never get any of those things. Emotional abuse is very insidious and damaging because we normally don't talk about it or treat it until it shows up as depression or other emotional disorder. Even then, we are more likely to drug the abused person to numb their pain instead of putting a stop to the abuse and providing therapeutic treatments to support their healing.

Aaron Beck's work on cognitive therapy, which I previously discussed, helps us understand the dynamics of depression. He observed that depressed patients all experience a sense of loss and feel that they are lacking something essential for their happiness. In Katlyn's case, that first major loss was clearly my leaving home. Beck explains that the traumatic triggering event most often leads to a pattern of distorted thoughts that revolve around 1) a negative concept of self, 2) a negative view of our world, and 3) a negative appraisal of our future.

Beck uses the term *loser* to describe the depressed person's self-assessment. In his mind, *He is a misfit—an inferior and inadequate being who is unable to meet his responsibilities and attain his goals.* Although I never saw Katlyn this way, I believe this is how she saw herself at times, especially given the continuing emotional stress she endured at home and school. Beck explains that the depressed person is predisposed to overreact to analogous conditions later in life. This is why professional therapy and a more loving, accepting environment would have been critically important for Katlyn to help her understand and heal the wounds that caused her depression.

Another branch of science that has led to greater understanding of ourselves is philosophy. The founders of Western philosophy, the Greeks, pioneered this ancient wisdom and left us with fundamental insights and practices that have greatly enhanced human understanding. Socrates, one of the leaders of Greek philosophy, was the first to seek the truth by persistent questioning, much like a therapist would do today. His questions would expose the underlying ignorance of people who thought they knew. This made him disruptive and highly controversial, even though he never claimed to have the answers to his questions.

Despite being controversial, Socrates believed that no one knowingly does wrong. His point was that if we knew in the fullest sense that something was wrong, we wouldn't do it. In his belief, then, learning virtues like kindness or acceptance was based on attaining sufficient knowledge and understanding. This is consistent with the idea that self-exploration is needed to gain sufficient understanding to change our negative thoughts and behaviors. As mentioned earlier, *when we know better, we do better*. For Socrates, the pursuit of inner knowledge and understanding was the same as pursuit of virtue; that is, it helps us learn how to become a better person.

In the end, local authorities arrested Socrates on charges of corrupting the young and not believing in the gods of the city. He was tried, convicted, and sentenced to die by poison. Socrates accepted his death sentence rather than agree to something he did not believe. If we consider that Socrates, a leading thinker of the times, was sentenced to death for asking questions, we see clearly how threatened we are by the truth. When it comes to our thoughts and behaviors that are motivated by internal doubts and insecurities, the last thing we want to see is the truth.

Understanding ourselves, or coming to self-realization in order to change the way we think and feel is not specifically addressed in Western religions. While all religions seek the same ends of love and acceptance as discussed in the last two chapters, the Western religions don't provide us with much direct guidance on how to get there, although prayer and worship can be very effective as they were for my mother. Eastern religions are different in this regard, as Buddhism and Hinduism provide very specific direction on how to train the mind to overcome our instincts and negative conditioning. The Buddha even used the metaphor of a wild elephant to describe the part of our mind that we need to bring under control.

The Buddha taught that suffering comes from our ignorance of the misperceptions and delusions of our mind. The way to free ourselves from suffering is to gain insight into the truth of our existence through mindfulness and meditation. His summary of the insights we need to recognize and experience are called the Four Nobel Truths:

1. There is suffering in life.
2. There is a cause of suffering, which is clinging to what we desire.
3. You can end your suffering by abandoning all craving.
4. The way to abandon craving is to choose correct thoughts, words, and actions.

The correct thoughts, words, and actions that the Buddha recommends are called the Noble Eightfold Path, which consists of Right View, Right Intention, Right Speech, Right Action, Right Livelihood, Right Effort, Right Mindfulness, and Right Concentration.

While the scope of the Buddha's teachings on how to change our minds and end our suffering go far beyond what could be discussed in this book, the wealth of scientific evidence on the benefits of mindfulness meditation confirm the wisdom of his teachings. The Buddha's idea that there is a right way to live, as exemplified in the Noble Eightfold Path, is also consistent with Western religious views on morality, such as specified in the Bible's Ten Commandments. We need not be concerned that the Buddha didn't teach of God in the way Western religions understand Him. Being raised in the Hindu tradition, the Buddha was taught to believe in a Universal Spirit that we are all part of, which resembles the Western concept of God. The Buddha claimed to have attained enlightenment, which is oneness with this Universal Spirit and all that exists, not unlike Jesus' claim that he was one with God. But in his own simple words, the Buddha said, *I teach only suffering and the end of suffering.* Working to bring an end to human suffering is a compassionate objective that is consistent with all other religions.

Science continues to document how mindfulness can help us to understand ourselves better. A March 2013 paper by Erika Carlson of Washington University in *Perspectives on Psychological Science* called, "Overcoming the Barriers to Self-Knowledge: Mindfulness as a Path to Seeing Yourself as You Really Are," states that research shows we have many blind spots when it comes to understanding our patterns of thinking, feeling, and behaving. She explores how self-knowledge can be improved by mindfulness—that is, paying attention to our thoughts and feelings in a non-judgmental manner. Her research indicates that people tend to overstate their virtues to hide their insecurities. However, non-judgmental observation, or mindfulness, can reduce our emotional resistance to feelings of inadequacy or low self-esteem. Getting to "non-judgment," then becomes the key to opening up to our insecurities. A therapist can help us with non-judgmental observation of our thoughts and feelings. Alternatively, both ancient wisdom and modern science suggest we could achieve this directly through meditation and mindfulness practice.

The Hindu faith has a focus on self-realization through yoga and meditation practices, just as the Buddha taught. The classical yoga texts reveal eight stages or "limbs" of yoga practice, only one of which is the yoga postures (asanas) popularized in the West. The first two stages are abstentions (Yamas) and observances (Niyamas). Like the Noble Eightfold Path, the Yamas and Niyamas provide moral guidelines. The Yamas (abstentions) of classical yoga are: Non-violence, Non-lying, Non-stealing, Non-sensuality (i.e. celibacy), and Non-greed. The Niyamas (observances) of yoga are: Purity, Contentment, Austerity, Study of the holy texts, and Attunement to God. The morality taught in classical yoga, like Buddhism, resembles the Western morality of the Bible's Ten Commandments, again pointing to the idea that ancient wisdom may collectively contain universal principles to live by.

Yogananda brought the Hindu teachings of Kriya Yoga to America in the mid-20th century. Like many Hindus, Yogananda was a disciple of Jesus' teachings and believed that love of God and our brother is man's greatest purpose in life. In a book of collected writings called *Man's Eternal Quest*, he presents an essay entitled "Self-Analysis: Key to the Mastery of Life." In this, Yogananda states, *Millions of people never analyze themselves... They don't know what or why they are seeking, nor why they never realize complete happiness and lasting satisfaction. By evading self-analysis, people go on being robots, conditioned by their environment. True self-analysis is the greatest art of progress....Find out what you are - not what you imagine you are! - because you want to make yourself what you ought to be. Most people don't change because they don't see their own faults.*

Chapter Summary

We previously discussed that all humans want and need love and acceptance. We know that to move toward greater love and acceptance in our lives, we must start with ourselves. The place to start is in our minds, examining our deepest thoughts and feelings, because this is what needs to change in order to release our negative ideas and become more loving and accepting, especially of ourselves. It sounds so simple. But our automatic defenses hide our pain and suffering from view. We are literally too afraid to look. Our mind has elaborate defense mechanisms to ensure that we remain in the dark.

Only when the pain becomes unbearable do we finally break down and seek help. At this point, the pain of looking more closely at our emotional suffering seems less than that of continuing on the same way. For most people, however, this point never comes. We find a way to muddle through life with the real source of our fears and anxieties hidden. We avoid the kind of self-examination that could lead to healing. We rarely meet a person that does not have underlying anxiety. They either show this outwardly or engage in some form of avoidance or distraction. Our greatest need then, in coming to love and acceptance, is for understanding of ourselves and our underlying fears and insecurities.

To undertake this type of self-examination, we need to feel safe. We cannot open up deep wounds when we feel threatened. One of the major problems we face is that those who have the greatest emotional wounds are often living in an environment where they remain under attack. The solution here becomes doubly difficult. And this often applies to our children who have no power to change their situation. My heart breaks over this, as I have seen up close the pain and suffering this brings. If you want to feel compassion for our human condition, just pause and think about the emotional abuse that we visit upon our pure and innocent children by yelling at them, and they upon each other, just as it was visited upon us by our parents. Where does this cycle of abuse end if not in greater compassion and understanding?

My emotional healing began when I made new friends and met spiritual teachers who could provide insight and understanding into my suffering from a context where I felt comfortable. Over time, because they were always compassionate, we built trust. This helped me feel safe enough to look at my deepest emotional wounds. Once I began to see the causes of my own suffering more clearly, I could better see Katlyn's. Just like love and acceptance, deeper understanding of ourselves is the first step to better understanding others. What Katlyn needed more than anything was first to feel safe and then to receive compassion and understanding for her own suffering. We all need this.

I tried hard to help Katlyn and gave her all the love I could, but this was not enough. She needed more kind and compassionate support at home. She also needed professional therapy or a counselor. My efforts to help in this regard were not successful because I could not force Katlyn to go to therapy and her mother would not agree to change her own behavior. Just as she had done with my sons, her mother accused me of poor parenting for not coming down harder on Katlyn. No doubt Katlyn lashed out in pain at her mother and was very difficult to get along with, particularly after she learned she had been misled about my love for her. However, this did not justify her mother responding in kind. Katlyn desperately needed help, starting with compassion, understanding, and acceptance at home. So all I could do was continue to love and support Katlyn the best I knew how.

Quite some time after my separation and divorce, Katlyn finally found the courage to cry out in pain and unleash her suffering on me, giving me the opportunity to see her like never before. I had left home because I didn't want my children to grow up and see me through their mother's angry eyes, but her mom continued to hold on to her anger and this was clearly put onto Katlyn despite my best efforts. My compassionate response to Katlyn's cry for help showed her the truth of my love for her and started our relationship on a healing path. I'll talk more about this in the next chapter on gratitude.

All I ever wanted for myself and my children was love and happiness. Truth is, that's all I ever wanted for their mother. In order to begin my healing and find the love within, I learned first hand how difficult, but important, it is to understand ourselves. I wished so often that I could help Katlyn feel safe, gain some understanding, and then find the goodness and love within herself as well. Katlyn also knew this is what she needed, as mentioned previously.

During the most difficult times of my separation from my children, I listened over and over to a song by Kenny Loggins from the album *Leap of Faith*, called "The Real Thing." The song was written to his young daughter during his separation and divorce. The chorus goes:

I did it for you, and the boys,
Because love should teach you joy,
And not the imitation,
That your mommy and daddy tried to show you.
I did it for you, and for me,
And because I still believe,
There's only one thing,
That you can never give up,
And never compromise on,
And that's the Real Thing you need in love.

Chapter 5

Gratitude

He is a wise man who does not grieve for the things which he has not, but rejoices for those which he has.

—Epictetus

When do we have enough? What do we really need to be happy? Is what we need outside there somewhere, or do we already have it? We've talked about our human need for love and acceptance, but we know that looking outside us for love can lead to suffering. Is it possible then, that we have everything we need to be happy right now? This is a popular notion that may be true. As a practical matter, however, this is not how most of us feel. And there are reasons.

Psychologists have discovered that humans have what is called a negative bias. That is, our brains process negative inputs faster and value them higher than positive ones. They believe much of this bias is evolutionary. When our species was competing for survival, it was more important to see and react to threats than opportunities. If an early human missed an opportunity for a meal, for example, chances were he would be okay. But if he missed a threat that he would become a meal, it was a different story.

This negative bias explains in part why it is so easy to be critical of ourselves and others. It also shows up in our relationships, as research shows it takes at least five positive interactions to make up for the harm caused by a single bad one. So focusing on the negative is part of being human. We are all pessimists by nature and this makes us prone to anxiety. As you might guess, dealing with this aspect of our mind takes us back to the elephant and the need for more retraining. This is what gratitude is about.

Martin Seligman, one of the founder's of Positive Psychology and author of the previously mentioned book, *Flourish*, has done extensive work on the benefits of practicing gratitude. In his book, he discusses the impact of two specific exercises, the Gratitude Visit and the What-Went-Well exercise. The Gratitude Visit starts with recalling someone from the past who has positively impacted our life for the better. The task is to write them a letter of thanks, then deliver it in person and read it to them aloud. This exercise forces us to recall a positive event in our life and helps to strengthen our relationship with the person responsible. In short, deliberately practicing gratitude upends our negative bias and makes us look at the positives in our life that we may have forgotten or taken for granted. Seligman's research shows that this simple exercise will make you happier and less depressed one month later. Think of that. Just one gratitude exercise could positively impact your life one month later.

The second exercise, What-Went-Well or Three Blessings as it is also called, asks us to set aside time just before bed to write down three things that went well each day and *why they went well.* The idea is to do this for at least one week. Acknowledging *why* they went well is just as important as *what* went well, as it makes us aware of good people or things responsible for our blessings. For people of faith, the "why" is often attributed to God's love for us, which helps us stay aware of His caring presence. The Three Blessings exercise has also been shown to have a profound positive effect on levels of happiness, including a measurable therapeutic effect in treating depression. Seligman reports that when these gratitude exercises were used in his college courses, students frequently reported they were *"life changing."* He states that if you do the What-Went-Well exercise for a week, you will likely still be doing it six months from now.

Why is gratitude so powerful? Is it just about changing our negative bias? Perhaps, but one would think such a strong instinctual drive would not be so easily reversed. If we think back to the last chapter, the rider does not usually retrain the elephant so quickly. My experience leads me to believe there may be something else at work. Practicing gratitude not only reminds us of positive events, but seeing why they happened opens up another level of awareness. We can see not only that good things happen to us, but also that good people in our life are responsible. We can see that many of the good things that happen to us are partly of our own creation. They come from friends we've made that value us. They come from relationships with our spouses, partners, friends and families that we've worked hard to nurture. They come from work and activities that reflect our talents and interests, and where we dedicate our time and efforts. At a subtle level, we can then recognize our own hand at work in creating our positive experiences and happiness.

For me, this could be one of gratitude's most profound effects—it helps remind us that we have goodness around us and *the power to create our own happiness*. When we experience this simply by observing our blessings and thinking about why, then we can come to know it, as the Buddha would say. Once we know it, we can begin to apply our power to choose wisely and create our own happiness. Alternatively, a negative bias by itself could lead us to believe there is no point in trying. We have no power and no control. Everything happens to us. We are just victims. Such feelings are common among the depressed. You can see how the application of these different viewpoints would lead us to create the exact opposite realities in our mind, and how practicing gratitude could help turn things around for a person who feels depressed and disempowered.

There's an old question about whether we see a glass as half-empty or half-full. The simple idea is that if you see it half-full, you're an optimist, see it half-empty and you're a pessimist. Our negative bias would lead most of us to see it half-empty. Upon deeper reflection, however, there is more to the question. Another relevant consideration is, "What were we expecting?" The next most important question is, "Do we have the power to refill the glass?" If a waitperson brings you a half-empty glass of water at a restaurant, you may be disappointed, even though you have enough to drink in the moment and could easily ask for more. If the same waiter brings a glass and a pitcher of water, fills your glass half-full, then leaves the pitcher on the table, you know he has provided you with all the water you could need. You just have to pour it yourself.

In this simple example, we can see the power of our expectations to create either happiness or disappointment. The half-full glass initially provided by the waiter was fine because we literally had what we needed (water) and could ask for more. It was only our comparison to what we could have had (a full glass) that made us unhappy. We know that if he provided the same amount of water in a smaller glass, the whole issue would not have surfaced. So our expectation creates a problem where no problem exists. Next, when we see that we have the power to obtain as much water as we need from the pitcher, even though our glass is still only half-full, there is no more problem.

Two important questions regarding life then might be, "What am I expecting and why?" and "What do I really need to be happy?" The expectation question illustrates that we all have desires that we compare to what we have. We don't normally ask the question why? We should remember how the media works to influence our desires and expectations to unrealistic levels in the hopes that we keep buying stuff. Our suffering can also come from expectations of ourselves and others that are not realistic. Therefore, asking why we have expectations and what we really need to be happy is important. Although we believe that things we *expect* or *desire* are actually things we *need* to be happy, research shows that after our basic survival and security needs are met, the poor are more happy than the rich. The real problem is often that we're holding out for champagne when all we really need is water.

Our ability to "refill the glass" also becomes key. Even when we have only a little of what we need, if we also have the ability to get more, we can be satisfied. The wisdom saying of, *Give a man a fish, you feed him for a day. Teach a man to fish, you feed him for a lifetime* applies to all of our needs. When we can create the conditions to meet our real needs, we feel empowered. Our happiness is then in our control. What hurts us, though, is we often don't see that there's a "water pitcher" right there in front of us. This is the real problem with negative bias. Not just that we see the glass as half-empty instead of half-full, but that we don't recognize we can fill our own glass and take the responsibility for doing so.

When we practice gratitude, then, we shift from the scarcity mentality of our negative bias, feeling "there's not enough" and "I'm a victim," to a feeling of empowerment, where "I have enough for now" and "I know how to create more." Of course, at one level, we all understand that humans have this capability. We know stories of people who have risen above incredible hardship to find happiness and fulfillment. But seeing this in another person and coming to know it for ourselves is different. When we practice gratitude and ask ourselves why, we can come to understand this creative power for ourselves. An analogous situation for me was that by simply recognizing my own kindness, I came to realize that the love I needed was within me. I'll describe this next and show how it relates to the power of gratitude to change us.

Just after Katlyn and I had our heart-to-heart discussion, I purchased a book called *Loving Kindness* by Sharon Salzberg that taught about the Buddha's Metta teachings I mentioned previously. One of the early passages that struck me was, *The foundation of the Metta practice is to know how to be our own friend. According to the Buddha, 'You can search throughout the entire universe for someone who is more deserving of your love and affection than you are yourself, and that person is not to be found anywhere. You yourself, as much as anybody in the entire universe, deserve your love and affection.'* Of course, this beautiful sentiment is almost incomprehensible for many of us, but it once again introduces the idea that self-love may be possible. Maybe we already have what we need to be happy. Could we really be that deserving? Is love and affection really inside of us and available to us?

One exercise in the *Loving-Kindness* book that helped me answer these questions was called "Remembering the Good within You." In it, we are asked to call to mind something *we have done or said that was a kind or good action, such as a time we were generous, or caring, or contributed to someone's well-being.* This is the flip side of gratitude. We could call it a "Generosity Exercise." It was a real eye-opener for me. I looked over the past year, wrote pages of good deeds in my journal, and concluded I had been much more kind and generous than I realized, even to myself. In Salzburg's words, *These reflections open us to a wellspring of happiness that may have been hidden from us before. Contemplating the goodness within ourselves is a classical meditation, done to bring light, joy, and rapture to the mind.*

Indeed, that was my experience. The idea that kindness and affection was within me, and could be given to myself as well as others, now seemed much more than a theory. I was beginning to experience and know the truth of the love that exists within me. The gratitude exercise is similar in that it awakens us to the goodness in our life and the idea that we have the ability to create and sustain such goodness. In other words, *we are as much the source of the positive experiences in our lives, as the recipients, in the same way that we can be the source of love.* These are very empowering realizations.

Practicing gratitude and remembering the good within me were both transformative exercises. They helped bring about the kind of self-realization that we spoke of in the last chapter, but more in the positive sense. That is, they help us to build strengths that lead to happiness and well-being, not eliminate problems that cause anxiety. Classic psychotherapy searches for the causes of our suffering, which are normally associated with overly negative and unrealistic thoughts and feelings about ourselves. The therapist presents more realistic and positive ways to think and invites us to change our minds. Positive psychology by contrast looks to build the capabilities and conditions that lead to happiness and well-being. This is also a mind-changing approach, but more focused on the positive thoughts and practices that show us how to create our happiness. For me, both approaches have merit. Working to change our negative thoughts while at the same time building positive capabilities and conditions is something I will return to later in the practice section of this book.

I was fortunate to experience the benefits of a gratitude exercise when Katlyn was a senior in high school, about six months after our emotional discussion. Her class had scheduled a weekend retreat and parents were invited to write a letter to their children. Below is the letter I wrote to Katlyn:

My Dear Sweet Katlyn (January 2008)

You began life as the perfect little girl, born just minutes after my 32nd birthday ended, more beautiful than any baby I had ever seen. Mom's labor was thankfully easy and short. That was such a loving and peaceful way to enter the world. It was an auspicious beginning, one that always indicated to me you were someone special.

You were such an adorable little girl. I treasured your greetings when I came home from work, yelling "Daddy, Daddy, Daddy" while wrapping your little arms around my legs at the doorway. To this day there is no better sound in my memory. As you grew, I remember cuddling with you, shaving with you, coaching your soccer teams, trips with Battye's class, Disney World, water skiing, etc. We played a lot and laughed a lot. It helped me rediscover the child in me.

So what kind of young lady have you grow into? As you have moved toward adulthood, your personal gifts have shown. The ones I admire the most are your kindness and compassion for others, your courage to do what you think is right, your work ethic and perseverance, and your humor and wit.

I list kindness and compassion first because to me, it is the most important. One thing you have in abundance is a loving heart, and there is no greater gift that God can give. You have always looked after those less fortunate and stood up for those who were condemned by others. This was the example set by Jesus, and I am so proud of you for choosing to follow that example by helping others.

Your courage is just as striking. It would be much easier for you to follow the crowd and do the things that some of your peers do. But you have chosen a more difficult path and you answer only to your own beliefs. This is a very rare quality and one that all true leaders possess. Having the courage of your conviction combined with a loving heart gives you the power to change the world.

Another wonderful quality that I personally identify with is your work ethic and perseverance. You've shown throughout your life the willingness to bust your butt to reach your goals, both in school and in sports. Things have not always come easy for you, but you never give up, and you always give it your best. I so admire that about you! From my experience, success in life comes more from effort, sacrifice, and perseverance than from raw brainpower or other gifts. So you should be able to do anything you set your mind to in life. Anything!

Lastly, what would life be without a little humor?? Not much fun at all, I think. You have the gift of a slightly twisted mind and an excellent ability to use words to make others laugh. And you have learned to laugh at yourself, because no one should take himself or herself too seriously. Thankfully, you have listened to one of my key pieces of worldly advice, "Don't be boring." You, my dear, will never be boring.

I also need to thank you for what you've taught me. You had the courage to share your deepest feelings about me last year. It helped break down a wall between us and showed me what I could do to be a better father. I will forever be grateful to you for that night and for the beautiful change in our relationship that resulted. You've also been great at working through challenges with your Mom and brothers. It's so hard growing up with all the pressures and stress you face, but you have made the effort to understand and be kind to your family, and it has helped a great deal. I'm glad I was able to be there and support you through it.

So, after all that, what are the most important words I want to leave you with?

First, I love and adore you with all my heart. I don't know how I could love you any more than I do. There is no one in the world more important to me than you.

Next, I admire you so much and I am so proud of you. I could not imagine a better daughter than you. Even though we all make mistakes, you're still perfect to me.

Remember that you can do whatever you set your mind to. Aim high. Try for the ridiculously awesome. The world needs people like you with courage and conviction that can make a big impact!

I will always be here for you, to support you and help you, no matter what happens. You may end up changing my diapers if I hang around long enough, but until then, I got your back!

I'll always be your Dad. And you'll always be my sweet little girl, my birthday present. You have been such a great gift to me. And it is such a privilege to be your Dad. Love you tons and tons!!! Xoxoxo... times a billon trillion.

I remember how much the letter meant to Katlyn. My words were hard for her to believe, but she knew I meant them and it helped us continue to build trust and affection. I know she felt empowered by my words as they spoke of her life choices and all the wonderful qualities she had developed. She was justifiably proud of herself. And I felt empowered, because there was a part of me reflected in all that was good in her. The old saying, "the apple does not fall far from the tree" is true.

I recently found the letter while searching through old papers from Katlyn. It gave me great comfort to know that I had told her exactly how I felt and that seven years later the letter still captured her perfectly. You may think I viewed her through the "rose-colored glasses" of a loving father, but I was not the only one who saw her that way. I shared the letter with one of Katlyn's dear friends about one month after her passing and he wrote,

I have been afraid to read your letter to Katlyn. I finally took the time to. I cried for ten days after Katlyn passed. I haven't cried since, until just now. And I'm still crying. Weeping like a little school girl. I wish I could have written her such a letter. Although from a little different angle I don't think I would have written many different words. She deserved your words.

While I was comforted on the one hand to find the letter and to hear how much it meant to her dear friend, it also reminded me of what an amazing person Katlyn was for so many and what a real tragedy it was to lose her. Also fortunate for me was finding a birthday card that Katlyn sent me nearly three years later in October 2010 while in her third year of college in Florida. In the card she had comprised her own gratitude letter for me:

Dear Dad,

I was so excited when I found this card because I think it really describes you and our relationship. I remember when I would sit on your lap and scream when you would give me whiskery kisses or poke a toothpick out of your mouth! You have always been the person I come to when I want to know something "daddy what's this?" To this day I still call you up asking random questions and you somehow always know the answers. I remember all the times you would help me with my school work. One time in particular was when you put all that work into helping me build that bridge for physics class.

I also remember we had a really big "heart to heart" when I was around 17. I called you in the middle of the night balling my eyes out and you came over. I remember I unloaded years of frustrations on you all at once. I told you about everything you had done that upset me in the past. After I told you, you went home and wrote everything down so you wouldn't forget. Then you promised me you were going to make everything on that list better. Dad you kept your promise and I think since that moment we have continued to grow closer. You have put sooo much effort into being a good father to me.

Soon after our talk I remember you came to my soccer game and brought me flowers. You even took me on a road trip to pick out a college! I also will never forget how you encouraged me to go to school here and you visited me for my birthday. I especially like the part in the card that says, "A love that has followed me mile after mile" even when those miles take me all the way to Florida.

I am so proud of you for being such a generous, humble, honest, hardworking, kind, and perseverant man. You work soooooo hard to give me the things you never had and to make my life a lot easier. Your hard work makes it possible for me to do my best in school, and work on becoming a better person, without having to worry about the things that a lot of other people worry about. I want you to know I never take you or the things and the money you give me for granted. I feel so lucky to have you as a father for soooo many reasons. My best memories and the times when I am the happiest are always the times when I'm with you and the boys. Love you Daddy and I hope you have a great birthday.

Katlyn's gratitude letter reminded me that we had made much progress since our emotional discussion years earlier when she called me a terrible father. It also illustrates a point made earlier, as I had not really changed. Our "relationship glass" was always half-full and we could have worked together at any point to fill it up. But she was just stuck in a view of our relationship that reflected her mother's ideas. Children follow their parent's example. And she believed I had abandoned her and no longer gave her the love she needed. In reality, I was right there trying to love her and she had just not given me a chance until that night she called me in tears.

By making it safe for her to vent her anger and promising to do my best to correct all the perceived mistakes, I helped her move from a victim mentality to one where she realized we could jointly create a better relationship. That one moment gave us a fresh start. I believe this is the real power of gratitude and generosity. It shows us that we can create what we need.

When our happiness depends on someone else, we are looking at life with our negative bias. It is disempowering, as we give responsibility for our happiness to others. While it's normal for a child to depend upon their parents, when two adults do this it's called co-dependency. This condition, as the name implies, is when each person depends on the other to fill their needs for love and affection. This type of exchange exists, at least in part, in most loving relationships as we look to fill our needs outside of ourselves. Remember, this is what we did as a child and the same pattern stays with us into adulthood. Interdependency is not necessarily a bad thing because when both adults have enough self-esteem, it can bring security and happiness to a relationship. However, when both are wounded and insecure, it normally leads to increasing levels of conflict or what is called a "love-hate" relationship.

My experience with my first wife was exactly that. We were both quite insecure, and so were highly motivated to get love and affection from each other. But because we were also very needy, neither could live up to the other's expectations. Then arguments would ensue where we would lash out at each other in pain. Hence, the love-hate bond. As time went on, our wounds got deeper and it became more of a "sex-hate" relationship. When I started to feel more love from my children and grew weary of arguments with my wife, my love-hate bond with her weakened. Once I would no longer respond to her criticism, my bond had effectively broken. Now all that was left in my mind was considering the best interests of our children.

In experiencing unconditional love and kindness with my children, I saw the goodness within myself, like the exercise mentioned above. I felt so grateful for them and saw my hand in creating our loving relationships. These realizations were very empowering for me. If I was capable of creating a pure, loving relationship with them, it made no sense to continue a love-hate relationship with my wife. She did not make this realization while we were together and after our separation she went in the opposite direction. She worked to manipulate my family in order to control me. I witnessed only anger and blame when we spoke about getting back together, though I had hoped our separation would lead her to self-reflection, compassion, and understanding, as it did for me.

We had started our marriage with very similar insecurities, but I found a way to grow in love and move away from our co-dependent relationship. If she had moved in the same direction, I would have kept on trying. While I was finding the love within me, she was moving deeper into negative thoughts and feelings of victimhood. She blamed me for everything and was unable to see how her own insecurities contributed to our problems. This is the fundamental difference between the positive, empowered view of happiness that we can create, and the negative, victim view of unhappiness that is forced upon us. And as both Katlyn and I demonstrated after our talk, happiness in a relationship is more of a choice than we think and we are responsible for the reality we create.

After my separation, I spent time talking with a friend and colleague from work. She was very kind and empathetic, which is what I needed more than anything at that moment. She knew I wanted to eventually go back home and always supported what was best for me and the kids. But after I concluded there was no hope of getting back together with my wife, we decided to consider a deeper relationship. This was risky, as we were both wounded from our previous relationships, plus we worked together, and my ex-wife blamed her for our split. As we had little to lose because we had already been judged, we decided to give it a try. I told her that all I wanted from a relationship was kindness and the freedom to be myself (i.e. please don't try to change me). She wanted the same, so despite the negativity all around us, it seemed like we had a basis to start.

Of course, it was not quite so simple. We each had major insecurities and both of our families made it difficult for us. But the wisdom of treating each other with kindness provided the environment we needed to work things out. We were friends first and committed to stay that way, even when we struggled. At times I felt angry because she did not give me enough love. Other times I felt afraid when I saw her emotional wounds and wanted to run away. She had similar feelings about me. But we were wise and patient enough to stay friends and continue working on ourselves.

We didn't raise our voices in anger, but were more likely to cry together over our pain. We each showed compassion for the other and this provided a safe environment for us both to heal.

Six years after I left home, we were married and thankfully still are, happily so. The difference in getting through our insecurities and relationship struggles, as compared to my first marriage, was that neither of us took the victim role and blamed the other. Likewise, neither tried to control the other. Co-dependency, at its worst, seeks to control the other person rather than look inside. No doubt we both wished we could make the other change at times. But we realized we were each responsible for our own happiness, even if we had not yet figured out how to get there. In time, our positive relationship beliefs became self-fulfilling. We believed in our own power to create happiness and because of that, we did. As we each healed and found our individual happiness, our relationship grew out of co-dependency and into authentic love.

It almost goes without saying that ancient wisdom supports the virtue of gratitude. The expression of gratitude is a primary focus for all major religions, including Christian, Muslim, Hindu, Buddhist, and Jewish faiths. Prayer and worship services commonly give gratitude to God or Spirit for our life and our blessings. The concept of gratitude is present in virtually all religious texts and rituals. As with love and kindness, the expression of gratitude is a universal religious sentiment.

Thomas Merton, an American Catholic monk and mystic was a prodigious writer and a proponent of interfaith understanding, pioneering dialogue with Eastern spiritual leaders including the Dalai Lama and Vietnamese Buddhist monk Thich Nhat Hanh. His views on the expression of gratitude are consistent with my own experience discussed earlier that as we give thanks for our blessings and ask the question "why," we gain a deeper awareness of the cause. In Merton's case, God's love for us is the "why" that we come to know. His thoughts on how we recognize and experience the love of God through gratitude are beautifully expressed on the following page:

To be grateful is to recognize the Love of God in everything He has given us—and He has given us everything. Every breath we draw is a gift of His love, every moment of existence is a grace, for it brings with it immense graces from Him.

Gratitude therefore takes nothing for granted, is never unresponsive, is constantly awakening to new wonder and to praise of the goodness of God. For the grateful person knows that God is good, not by hearsay but by experience. And that is what makes all the difference.

There is another important aspect of faith and gratitude that Merton is making. We are grateful to God not because He will answer our prayers, but because He already has. Through faith, we recognize that we have everything we need in the moment. If God wanted us to have something different, it would be so. What God has given us, then, is the power to gratefully accept His gifts and create the life we desire with them.

The Islamic Quran also encourages followers to be grateful to God for His blessings in daily prayers and during fasting. Muhammad states, *Gratitude for the abundance you have received is the best insurance that the abundance will continue.* While many religions like Islam teach us to be grateful to God so our blessings will continue, the Buddha teaches us to be grateful because things could always be worse: *Let us rise up and be thankful, for if we didn't learn a lot today, at least we learned a little, and if we didn't learn a little, at least we didn't get sick, and if we got sick, at least we didn't die; so, let us all be thankful.* There is also a Chinese proverb that states, *When eating bamboo sprouts, remember the man who planted them.* Although there may be different motivations, the idea of gratitude as an important virtue is deeply rooted in all religious traditions and ancient wisdom.

Chapter Summary

We've discussed our human need for love and acceptance, and the importance of understanding our deep insecurities in order to help change our negative thoughts and feelings about ourselves and our lives. This is difficult because we have sophisticated defense mechanisms along with a built-in negative bias. We are pessimists by nature. Our emphasis on the negative aspects of life can make us feel like there is little we can do to help ourselves. In short, we often feel like victims.

In past chapters, we discussed how therapy, meditation, journaling and prayer can help us change our negative thoughts and feelings, once we find the compassion and strength to look at them. This chapter focused more on a positive approach to changing our mind by creating the awareness and conditions for our own happiness. Practicing gratitude is one such approach that has been demonstrated to have profound positive impact on our feelings of well-being, while also relieving feelings of anxiety and depression.

One benefit of practicing gratitude is that it immediately shifts our negative bias and helps us to look at the positives in our lives. This by itself is beneficial as it reminds us there is a different way of seeing the world. When we take a further step and ask why or how the people and things we're grateful for have come into our lives, we become more aware of our own creative power and for some, the creative power and love of God. My personal experience with gratitude and generosity practices suggests that they not only help us build awareness of our blessings, but also remind us of the goodness we have inside and our own power to create happiness.

Other important questions that arise as we think about gratitude or the lack thereof are, *What am I expecting and why?* and, *What do I need to be happy?* In our search for happiness and well-being, these questions are not trivial. Our simple discussion around the glass of water being half-empty or half-full reminds us how powerful our expectations are and how often our unconscious thoughts and desires serve to limit our happiness when there really is no problem. When we are feeling disappointed, these questions are a good place to start in turning that feeling around.

The different experiences I had between my first and second marriages demonstrated how a positive, empowered view of happiness that we can create, compares to the negative, victim view of unhappiness that is forced upon us. In both cases, I brought major insecurities into the relationship, as did my spouses. In my second marriage, our mutual commitment to kindness and friendship, along with the belief that we were each responsible for our own happiness, were key. In the absence of anger and blame, we created a safe place and gave each other time to get the emotional healing we needed.

My relationship with Katlyn also experienced a significant shift in part because of the gratitude we each expressed for the other. The change became possible when she released her negative, victim based view of our relationship and embraced a positive view that together we had the power to create something wonderful. But her emotional wounds had been created over many years and would not be so easily healed. I'll talk more about Katlyn's life and how I have come to understand her choices in the upcoming chapter titled, *For the Love of Katlyn.*

One of Katlyn's dearest loves had this beautiful expression of gratitude to offer her after her passing:

You have forever changed my life. You were my light in the darkness shining bright. The world is truly not the same without you. You were my best friend, inspiration, confidant, and partner. You paddled into my life one day and have forever changed who I am. Through your love, prayers, and unwavering support you helped me through some of my life's hardest battles. I thank God for every second I was blessed to spend with you.

Chapter 6

Humility

Humility is the mother of all virtues;...
It is in being humble that our love becomes real,...

—Mother Teresa

Humility is defined as *a modest view of one's own importance;* that is, with humility, we don't think we are better than others or put ourselves above them. Growing up in a family of thirteen children, this principle was drilled into me regularly. The minute one of us would step out of line and think we were something special, the rest of the clan would pile on (verbally, physically, or both) and put us back in our place. This had quite a useful purpose, because with all of us crowded into a small 5-bedroom home, we could hardly afford to have any "special" people around. We needed to be sensitive to the wants and needs of those around us and learn to work out our differences, even if the process of working things out was not always pretty.

Another example of humility that profoundly influenced my early life was my father Ernest. He grew up on a small farm and joined the US Army near the end of World War II. There he learned to repair motor vehicles and decided to open his own auto repair shop, called *Ernie's Garage*, shortly after the war ended. I began working with him at the garage in my early teens. Within just a few short years, he had taught me how to do every type of auto repair performed in the shop, never answering my questions directly but instead responding by asking me questions. Like a Master teacher, he did not tell me what to do. Instead, his patient questioning would slowly develop within me the ability to find my own answers. This was his humility in practice.

In my late teens, I witnessed another example of the power of my father's kind and humble approach. He not only performed auto repairs at a very affordable price, but would also allow customers to slowly make payments on their outstanding bills as they were able. As a result, he had a large pile of unpaid bills in his desk even though he barely had the money to pay his own bills. His humble devotion to his customer's best interest was returned to him one summer when the garage accidentally caught fire and burned to the ground. I remember coming home just as the fire was put out to see my father sitting on the ground on the hill looking down over the destroyed building with tears in his eyes, surely wondering what he would do now to feed his family. He did not have fire insurance because with fifteen mouths to feed, insurance was not an affordable option. But his loyal customers and friends from our small town came out in droves the next day with donations of time and money to help clean up the destroyed building and build us a new one. Within a month we had a beautiful new garage that was so much better than the old one. This was only possible because the humble service my father and mother had always given to others was returned to us in our time of need. That was our insurance.

The importance of humility seems to be lost on our modern society. Several years ago a respected colleague of mine from work told me about an exciting experience he and his family had over the weekend at a local Christian church. He said the pastor had provided a moving sermon that was quite inspirational. My long spiritual quest had made me somewhat skeptical of inspirational church speakers, so I asked him, *Do you think the pastor is a holy man or just a good performer?* He paused thoughtfully and then said, *I really don't know.* The next day he told me he wished that I had never asked him the question. Some months later, the same pastor was dismissed from the church for having an extramarital affair with a woman who worked in the church office who was also married. At this point, we both had the answer to my question.

This example illustrates some important points about humility or the lack thereof, and how it gets us in trouble. First let's take my colleague. What was he looking for and why did this type of preacher appeal to him? If we start at the beginning, we know that as children we were told how to think and act by our parents and those in authority. We may have learned more by example, but we are still used to being told what to do. In school, this pattern continued. Then in work, guess what? We're still told how to think and act by those in charge. "Being told" is the primary method used for teaching and it's where most of us are comfortable. This is why we flock to hear the charismatic teachers who speak as though they have great wisdom and authority. We defer to them, as though they are better than us, and they assume the role of superiority. In a sense, we are humbling ourselves before them. This kind of humility is not helpful, however, because we are still not learning how to think and act for ourselves.

Now let's examine the pastor's role. When someone speaks with self-confidence and authority, we tend to find them believable. Yet if we consider how the Master teachers taught, they used three primary methods: first they taught by their own example, next using observations, stories or parables, and lastly by asking questions. Jesus, the Buddha, and Socrates, for example, all used these methods. Even when the Buddha revealed teachings like the Four Noble Truths, he said please don't take my word for it. You need to experience it for yourself to know the truth. This is why he also taught meditation. Showing examples, telling stories, and asking questions help us begin to have the experience directly so we can come to our own understanding. Simply telling someone the truth as we understand it and expecting them to accept it without question literally stunts their growth. According to a *New York Times* opinion piece called "Make School a Democracy," by David L. Kirp, some educators have recognized this fact and begun the shift toward more experiential and application based learning.

The charismatic teacher who uses methods that call attention to himself demonstrates a lack of humility and lack of awareness of what we need to learn. This does not help us experience the truth, but instead uses the opportunity to elevate himself. The truth has its own power. It does not need to be shouted or dramatically delivered. In fact, Master teachers all recognized the danger in being idolized and put on a pedestal. For example, in the Gospel of John, Jesus says, *The words I speak are not my own, but my Father who lives in me does his work through me.* The Buddha and Socrates did not teach by profound declarations of truth, but said we should consider their ideas and questions for ourselves in order to come to the truth. The Master teachers did not try to become our guru because they realized we need to find our own inner truth.

This chapter on humility, then, takes a little different approach from previous chapters by demonstrating that our self-awareness can help us to better understand where others are coming from. We have discussed our core needs for love and acceptance, how difficult it is to come to greater self-awareness and healing, and how gratitude can help change our outlook on life by showing us our positive creative power. As we begin this self-transformation, we start to observe the dynamics of the world around us with the same deeper understanding. When we become aware of our own insecurities and how we hide from them and fool ourselves, then the motivations of the people and leaders we interact with become clearer, like the preacher discussed above. If we learn to practice love and kindness, acceptance, understanding, and gratitude, we will gain humility for ourselves. Our focus in this chapter is more on understanding the people who influence our lives, particularly our friends, teachers, and leaders, because with this greater understanding we could choose and interact with them more wisely.

What is the charismatic teacher's real motivation, then, when he seeks to call attention to himself? In a word, "self-gratification." It helps boost his ego, or opinion of himself. When we go see such teachers and listen to their wisdom, they act as though they are better than us and we go along with it, which makes them feel good. This is why they are on a stage or altar above us. We look up to them and give them our admiration and money, so why wouldn't they feel good? And their dramatic performances play right into this relationship. Unfortunately, though such individuals can be very talented, their work is often motivated by their lack of self-esteem and their need for attention. It's not about us; it's about them and their needs. Not that their words aren't beautiful. In the case of religious teachers, we instinctively recognize their words as true. After all, they are normally repeating teachings of the Masters. But their methods expose their true motivations. This is why I asked my colleague the question about his charismatic pastor.

Master teachers, by contrast, uniformly demonstrated humility. They never put themselves above anyone. They taught at the same level of their students, normally being surrounded by them. They didn't use dramatic presentations, but taught simply and experientially as mentioned above. The ego-driven teacher says, *I am the light. I will shine my light upon you and heal you.* The Master teacher says, *I can see the light within you and I will help you find it so you can heal yourself.* The Masters recognized that we all have the same inner wisdom and that all human mistakes have the same cause. We harm others only because we are wounded and confused. Once we realize these truths, we know better than to put ourselves above others. Most of our modern day teachers and leaders have not yet attained this level of understanding and humility.

This explains how the pastor can preach about the Bible, then behave the opposite to his own teachings. This demonstrates that his primary motivation was self-gratification; that is, serving his own needs and desires. If he were primarily concerned with living the Bible's teachings, or with serving his congregation, or even the well-being of his office worker, he would not have chosen a secret and dishonest affair. We see this nearly everyday among our leaders; for example, the pedophile priest who abuses an altar boy or the elected official who embezzles public money. They don't "walk the talk," as the saying goes. How do these people in important positions of power and trust live with themselves, you might ask? Because this behavior is so prevalent, there must be an explanation. Modern science has found one. It's called *confabulation.*

Research shows that our conscious mind is very skilled at fabricating reasons to explain the path our subconscious desires want to take. We invent convincing explanations for our behavior, even when we have no knowledge of what is actually motivating us. We justify our every thought and action, sometimes even crafting heroic stories about the most grievous acts. This is what would make the cheating pastor say, for example, *She was a lost soul and I was just showing her the love of God.* The embezzling elected official might think, *I have brought so much good to my district. I have earned this money.* They don't believe they are doing any wrong. When you believe you are better than others, you also believe you're above the rules. We are able to *confabulate* our own rules and explanations to justify our hidden desires, while still remaining clueless.

When you put this all together, you can see how we could create a mess of our world. In summary, we are drawn to ego-driven leaders who are outwardly confident and authoritative, but they are often very insecure. That is, their confidence is just an act. They are skilled at playing us, mostly by tapping into our hidden fears and insecurities, which is easy for them because they have the same ones. They pretend to be working for us and in many cases they believe this, but they consider themselves above us and are primarily motivated by their own desires and need for self-gratification. They confabulate stories to convince themselves differently, and we accept those stories, as we also want to believe we are better than others and on a noble quest of right against wrong. The real danger, then, is not that our leaders believe they're better than everyone else and fabricate stories to prove it, but that they sweep us and our insecurities along with them.

History is full of examples to illustrate this danger such as the Holocaust in World War II, the Catholic Crusades, and early American justification of slavery and taking land from the natives. Today it is obvious that a country founded on the *self-evident* noble truth that *all men are created equal,* had made an unwritten exception at the time for African and Native American people, and of course all women. They only meant *all men* after you exclude over half of them. Ironically, the person who wrote those words, Thomas Jefferson, owned a large number of slaves at the time. Talk about confabulation. Don't get me wrong. I love America and the ideals it was founded upon. And we've recognized these mistakes over time, even if we haven't yet fully corrected them. We just need to understand how they happen if we want a better life and better world. When many of the greatest leaders and best minds throughout human history have been sadly mistaken, why would we want anything but humble and open-minded leaders? We choose the ego-centric types only because they reflect our own insecurities and fears.

There are humble and open-minded leaders out there, but they are unfortunately rare. They don't project the kind of self-confidence and authority that is more common, so they often don't gain the followers, as we are used to being told what to think and do. They literally come from a place of love and are looking primarily to serve others. They don't use us to get something for themselves and don't prey on our fears, but instead demonstrate their humility through compassion and understanding. They treat everyone with respect because they consider every being as their equal. They are excellent listeners and would rather hear about you than talk about themselves. The reason we may not recognize them is they most often stay "down in the grass" and don't call attention to themselves. We feel good around them, but they are not in the authoritative leadership mold to which we are accustomed.

The same can be observed in our personal relationships. Real love comes from a place of humility, as the Mother Teresa quote states at the beginning of this chapter, and may be difficult for us to recognize. However, a person with a humble heart and coming from a place of love can instantly recognize the same in another by the light in their eyes and expression on their face. There is a gentleness about them. When we're in a place of fear, however, we can miss this or feel threatened by it. If you have ever been smiled at by a stranger in a public place, you may have felt this discomfort. We feel like they are acting strange or maybe after something, when their smile could just be a simple offer of kindness.

But even a young child will go to the arms of a stranger if they recognize this light and love within them. Katlyn would call me the "baby whisperer" as I have that attraction to children and they to me. When I see a pure and innocent child before me, that child seems to call forth the same innocent child within me. This childlike love and pure innocence was also clearly visible in Katlyn. One of her friends spoke for many of us when he called her, *The most beautiful person ever.* This is what we can see in another person when we are looking with a humble and loving heart.

By contrast, a person who is filled with fear and judgment can project those fears on the most innocent of souls. Suicide bombings of civilians, including women and children, by religious extremists demonstrate this truth. They are often carried out by disaffected youth who are brainwashed into such acts, with their leaders feeding on their anger and promising them great rewards in heaven. Yet it is not the leaders that sacrifice their lives for these heavenly rewards. They are not "walking the talk," which tells us all we need to know about the sincerity of their teachings. And as horrifying as such terrorist acts are, the underlying motivations for such acts are more prevalent than we would like to admit.

Those of us who harbor strong beliefs of good and evil would do well to consider how different we are from these extremists. Is wishing harm or even death upon the "evil" someone that we perceive really that different than killing them? Is this really what our Master teachers taught? Tom Koch, in a *New York Times* opinion piece entitled, "What's Worse Than Sad" had this to say:

Our tragedy is this collective, fatal flaw, which insists on demonizing those we disagree with and turning them into mortal enemies. From this extreme judgmental perspective, then, we seek to eliminate what we define as evil and any means can be justified. Alternatively, when we come from a place of humility and compassion, we seek to help those who are confused or mistaken. Therein lies the difference.

From our observations, we can see that the extreme self-righteous people of all religions and creeds, by their own thoughts and actions, often create the very evil that they preach against. Research confirms that in order to create mass atrocities, you need to have extreme overconfidence and believe you have a moral mandate. We should have great compassion for the children and young adults who are led by such individuals and indoctrinated into these hateful beliefs. Such beliefs are also adopted by people later in life, especially those that are the most angry or insecure. This appears to be a case of "willful ignorance," as they literally know better. But when we are angry and have experienced great injustice, then hear a story of good and evil that fills us with pride and self-righteousness, it can be too good to resist, even though it requires us to block out common sense we already possess. As the expression goes, we willingly "drink the Kool-Aid."

I have a sister who adopted extreme evangelical Christian beliefs later in life, one of the same siblings that helped convert Katlyn's mother to these beliefs after our separation. At one point, she approached my mother with her Bible and told her that if she had sufficient faith, my mother could heal her badly worn and painful hips. My sister was there to help my mother with this miracle. For the rest of our family, the idea that she could help my mother heal miraculously by showing her how to have greater faith was absurd. Even if this were physiologically possible, my mother lived her whole life of service based on faith in God. She was the example we all tried to emulate. In this situation, my sister had clearly lost the common sense she once had and seemed to be suffering from *delusions of grandeur,* which are ideas humans *confabulate* to boost their self-esteem.

We adopt such ideas because performing a miracle in the name of God is the ultimate in demonstrating our self-worth. What could be more gratifying to our wounded ego? We convince ourselves we are acting in the name of God and out of love for others, but this explanation does not pass the common sense test. At the root of my sister's transformation was an ego-centered preacher preying on her insecurities. This preacher was not much different than the televangelist on TV that says, *Send me your money, then touch the TV screen and you will be healed.* Her preacher's approach was just a little more sophisticated and less obvious.

When we finally convinced my mother to see a doctor about her hips, he said the normal ball in her hip joint had been worn down to a mushroom shape. The doctor had seen this condition in books but never thought he would meet a person who could bear such pain for so long. That was her true faith on display, something the rest of us never doubted. My mother, of course, did not pray for a miracle cure and instead had successful hip replacement surgery. But some people get caught up in looking for such miracles and fail to take action that could bring about their own healing. Unfortunately, this was true of Katlyn, unbeknownst to me at the time. I'll talk more about that later.

If we are very angry or insecure then the perfect home for us is an extreme self-righteous group that follows an infallible scripture and takes their direction from the one and only true God. We should not single out any particular religion, as there are modern day examples of this phenomenon in all religions. And we should recognize that it is the *incorrect* interpretation of religious teachings that lead one to extreme self righteousness, as opposed to humility, which is what many churches practice and what all Master teachers demonstrated. But once we adopt these extreme righteous moral beliefs, we believe that we are special, protected by God, and not capable of doing wrong. This is the perfect defense for our insecurity and the perfect justification for any manner of judgment or immoral act toward our perceived enemies.

My experience with religion and churches is they attract us in two ways. First, they preach the loving teachings of our Masters that we instinctively know are true. At the same time, they prey on our egos and insecurities to manipulate and control us. They tell us God loves us, but we must follow *them* to be saved and get to heaven. Otherwise, we are doomed to suffer in hell. They tell us we are children of God, but also not worthy (i.e. sinners) in the eyes of God. They fill us up with self-righteousness and tell us we are better than those who don't share our beliefs. Then they offer us forgiveness for all our sins because we're not that good after all. And don't step out of line or question their teachings, because you will immediately become an outcast. Compassion and forgiveness will have left the building. My divorce taught me that. When we stand back and read this description, it does not really make sense.

Please don't take offense if you have found a religion or church that is true to your Master's loving and humble teachings. My experience above is limited, but may be more common than many church-goers would like to admit. Still, when we seek to grow in love, acceptance, and understanding, we can benefit greatly from communities of like-minded individuals. For many, this describes their church or spiritual community. And for churches that look more like my experience described above, they might benefit from reconsidering the humble example and loving intentions of their Master teacher, not necessarily the exact words in their holy scriptures or church dogma, because these things are often in conflict.

For those who interpret their holy scriptures literally, there are good reasons to reconsider this practice. Remember that our scriptures were not written by our Master teachers, but passed down verbally for in many cases hundreds of years, and then written as best they could be remembered and understood by humans who were not at the level of the Master. This would be like a college lecture that was passed down verbally for a hundred years by some school children, and then written down. The children split up over the generations, so different versions of the same lesson are written. Later another group of the children get together and decide what parts of the writings we should keep and what should be disregarded. Then finally we translate these writings into a different language just to further cloud the meaning. In such a case, we would all understand if the lesson had changed somewhat or reflected the limited consciousness of the children along with the original intentions of the teacher. We certainly would not treat every word as though it came directly from the teacher's mouth.

Let us also acknowledge that this pattern of extreme self-righteous behavior is present everywhere in the world, not just limited to religions. Look at political parties and you will see exactly the same dynamic around their particular agenda or creed and the way they demonize their opposition. We certainly see this pattern of extreme self-righteousness all over the internet and on cable TV. Vitriolic speech against the opposition is associated with almost every belief or cause. As much as we value freedom of speech, we might be better off with freedom *from* speech, as this type of speech only incites intolerance and hatred. We can even witness this behavior in professional sports, with fans sometimes killing one another while rioting after a particular game. Think about that...killing other sports fans from hatred over the outcome of a game.

In truth, we all behave self-righteously. It's just a matter of degrees. We *marginalize* others who we disagree with or judge unworthy. Racism is an obvious example. In more extreme cases, we *dehumanize* them and could care less about their struggles and suffering. This explains how we can have so many poor people in such a wealthy world. At worst, we *demonize* others we perceive as evil and wish them harm or hurt them directly. We are so right and they are so wrong, that we choose violence and war as the only solution. It is frightening to see our highest leaders sometimes behave in this extreme self-righteous manner. But it is still the wounded and angry child within us who spews the hate, casts the stone, strikes the blow, wields the sword, or fires the weapon.

We can see that self-righteousness, or the need to be right and feel better than others, is a fundamental human response to feelings of anger, unworthiness and our unmet desire for love and acceptance. Therefore, we should view this human condition with compassion and understand that the extreme self-righteous need help. The clear solution is to learn humility, that is, learn to treat all others with respect as our equals. But like the virtues of love and acceptance discussed earlier, learning humility requires compassion, understanding, and in many cases healing. There is no short cut.

Research in the social sciences confirms that humility is hard to achieve. It shows that when we want to believe something is true, our conscious mind is very skilled at finding reasons to support it. We think we're being objective, but instead we seize upon any rationale to support our preconceived ideas and purposely ignore disconfirming evidence. This is particularly true in the way we see ourselves. We have a strong tendency to overstate our virtues, though we tend to see the faults of others very clearly. We remain unaware of our faults and self-serving biases, particularly in situations involving disagreement or conflict. Because of our bias toward our preexisting beliefs, science tells us that we can best learn from those who disagree with us. But even when faced with evidence to the contrary, we rarely adjust our opinions or overly positive views of ourselves. This is why human conflicts often escalate even when people on the outside can readily identify the mutual fault among parties along with potential solutions.

For purposes of this chapter, then, it may be helpful to further define what is meant by humility. First, humility means that we respect others as equals and don't put ourselves above them or below them. Next, with humility, we don't put our needs ahead of others. We care equally about their wants and needs. This would lead us away from self-gratification, especially at someone else's expense. Lastly, we don't value our own opinion above others because we realize that we have an internal bias in favor of our own beliefs and our own virtues, and therefore cannot possibly be objective about anything. Therefore, we not only respect the opinions of others, we seek them out. A defining characteristic of the humble person is their ability to listen without their own agenda. They are fully present for you when you speak and there is no rush to voice their own opinion. They want to understand what you think and how you feel.

We have noted Maya Angelou's famous words, "when we know better, we do better." But the humble person knows that none of us has reached our full potential and that we can always do better. These statements appear to be in conflict, but both are true. With humility, we remain aware of our limited knowledge and understanding. Therefore a humble person never stops trying to learn and improve. Coming to "know better" so we can "do better" is not a passive process brought about simply by living. It is hard work. This is why the humble person keeps an open mind and never stops searching for greater knowledge and understanding. Once we think we have it all figured out, our learning and growth stop, and we often regress.

It's important not to confuse humility with low self-esteem, which can express itself in two ways, both passively and aggressively. Remember, when the elephant feels threatened, it either runs away (passive) or attacks (aggressive). Passively it may show up as a lack of confidence, quietness, or inability to look someone in the eye; aggressively it shows itself as over-confidence, pride, and self-righteousness. Although they appear as opposites, the underlying issue is the same, as in two sides of the same coin. And just to be clear, outwardly self-confident people normally don't know they are insecure. The more confident they try to appear, the more likely they are insecure. Unfortunately, those who most need to realize this truth are the least likely to do so. I know, as I was one of the outwardly confident ones and it took a lot of pain and suffering to help me see my true motivations.

Therefore, we should not mistake outward confidence of others (or ourselves) as a sign of strength, as it is often the opposite. Those who are truly strong and secure within themselves have no need to prove they are right, but instead are open to learning from others. They retain a *healthy self-doubt,* which is the opposite of *self-righteousness,* because they realize their knowledge and perspective is limited, and that we can always benefit from a different perspective and gain a greater understanding. They do not project their confidence outwardly. Their strength shows itself as a calm presence. Even though they may have clear beliefs, they don't need to convince others. They may stand firmly in their truth, having the *courage of their convictions,* but are open to other points of view and are not threatened if others disagree. In a word, they are humble, which does not mean they feel lesser, as in the sense that they would bow down before others. With true humility, we see all people as equals and therefore, equally deserving of honor and respect.

For those whose insecurities show up as lack of confidence or shyness, it's never good to hold ourselves below others. Our feelings of unworthiness are mistaken. They were mistakenly taught to us by our parents or others who were likely taught the same. Though our society and the people we encounter often reinforce this feeling, they do this only because they are suffering in the same way. We are all equally worthy of love and acceptance as we are. Recognizing this fact is the goal of our inner work. When others project superiority, they are also mistaken and it is only their insecurities and lack of understanding that makes them do so. While it is correct to respect our parents, teachers, leaders, and elders, it is not necessary or helpful to consider ourselves below them. We look up to them with gratitude for their support, wisdom, and understanding, but we are equally deserving of respect. Overcoming our lack of self-confidence, however, is not easy and requires the type of inner work we have been discussing.

Pride, like self-confidence, is a quality that we generally view as positive, as in taking pride in our country or work. There is an aspect of pride, however, that makes us feel better than others and keeps us from seeing our faults. The old proverb that *pride goeth before a fall* is a helpful warning. Pride can also help us cover up underlying feelings of low self-esteem. An alternative to pride is feeling a sense of accomplishment along with gratitude for everything that helped us along the way. For example, we rightly feel a sense of accomplishment when we achieve a goal that we have worked for long and hard. But instead of filling ourselves with pride and feeling better than others, we could recognize our hard work and be grateful for the role our parents, teachers, families, coworkers, and friends played influencing and supporting us. We could also be thankful for our good mind and body, or the good fortune we've had to be born into these circumstances. It doesn't take much effort to recognize we're only partly responsible for our successes. There is often a great deal of help or good fortune involved. When we are prideful, though, we can take all the credit and put ourselves above others.

Another reason humility is important is that different beliefs are what separate us. It's obvious that our need to defend our different beliefs is a major source of human conflict. Because we are insecure, we have a need to be right. We become stubborn and try to convince others they are wrong because our self-esteem is threatened by their disagreement. As humans, we readily find reasons to justify our opinions and fail to see our own faults. The more insecure we are, the more likely we are to judge others harshly, then use this to justify all manner of grievous thoughts and behaviors against them. While real injustices exist everywhere, the involved parties usually have very different beliefs about who is at fault, and resorting to arguments and violence as a path to resolution more often makes the situation worse.

We previously discussed how developing compassion, acceptance, and understanding for our own insecurities can help us see things differently. Once we do, we can accept that people have different beliefs and give them our respect just the same. When we seek to resolve our differences from this perspective, everyone can feel safe and lasting resolutions become possible. This is humility in practice. John Mayer has a song titled *Belief* that speaks to the danger of holding on to our beliefs without humility. The lyrics, in part go:

Oh, everyone believes,
And no one's going quietly,
We're never gonna win the world,
We're never gonna stop the war,
We're never gonna beat this if belief is what we're fighting for

There is another song by Mac Davis called *Oh Lord It's Hard to Be Humble* that also shows the difficulty in learning humility. The first line goes, *Oh Lord it's hard to be humble when you're perfect in every way.* This line succinctly states our problem. We want to feel perfect in every way, which leads us to overstate our virtues and put ourselves above others. But we also need to practice humility and treat others as equals if we want to resolve our differences and have some peace in our world.

When we were newborns, we most likely felt *perfect in every way* in the arms of our parents. As we grew up, we struggled in our judgmental world to find that feeling again. So our mind creates stories to help us feel better about ourselves and at the same time judge others, though this is not a cure for what ails us. The real cure is love and connection to others. In the end, we need to bring awareness and compassion to our human condition, and understand our deepest pains and motivations. Then we can begin to find the love we need inside along with true self-esteem. We may someday again feel *perfect in every way,* but this would not be our ego talking. It would come from the real love we find in our hearts. Ultimately, the path to self-realization and self-love brings us to the humility we need to get along with our brothers and sisters.

Modern society does not teach us humility, but primarily narcissism; that is, that life is all about *me me me,* as Katlyn said. This just reinforces our natural tendency to be self-absorbed. Fortunately history provides many examples of the beauty of humility and its power to change the world. In fact, it would not be a stretch to say that the greatest teachers and leaders of all-time, those that had the greatest influence on mankind, have been humble. If we look back at Master teachers mentioned earlier—Jesus, the Buddha, and Socrates—they all demonstrated humility, unlike other leaders of their time. They had no money or possessions, no churches or armies, and very little status. Two of them were even put to death. Yet, the truth of their humble lives and teachings profoundly influence us still today.

Mahatma Gandhi, the great sage who used non-violent resistance to lead 400 million Indians out of bondage under the British Empire, is another example of the power of humility. He started out as a shy lawyer who failed at everything he tried, but somehow grew to profoundly influence the largest country on earth. Stephen Cope, in his book called *The Great Work of Your Life,* shows how Gandhi's transformation came from his devotion to and practice of principles in the sacred Hindu text, the *Bhagavad Gita*. Cope says, *Gandhi came to believe that any power he might have to affect the world only emerged when he got himself out of the way, and let God do the work.* Gandhi wrote, *There comes a time when an individual becomes irresistible and his action becomes all-pervasive in its effects. This comes when he reduces himself to zero.* Gandhi's humility before God was reflected in his outward humility toward mankind.

If you search the internet for the greatest United States president, you'll find that Abraham Lincoln most often tops the lists of American historians and scholars. He would likely top a list of the most humble as well. Like Gandhi, Lincoln grew up poor and became a shy, country lawyer. He was entirely self-educated and lost more elections than he won. As an unlikely President, Lincoln filled his administration with adversaries, not a bunch of yes-men, as he was more concerned with doing the best possible job than serving his own ego. His unwavering belief in the Constitution's words, "all men are created equal," led him to abolish slavery while still holding the fragile country together through a long and bloody Civil War. In his second inaugural address, Lincoln spoke not as a triumphant victor, but as a humble servant. On the need to reconcile with the South and rebuild the Union, he advised that we proceed, *With malice toward none; with charity for all.* Lincoln never characterized Southerners as evil or as mortal enemies, even during war.

Nelson Mandela, the first democratically elected President of South Africa, was one of the few modern leaders to demonstrate a similar humility. He had spent 27 years in prison only to lead his country's transition from all-white rule to democratic rule by the black majority. What made Mandela so successful was he did not take the opportunity to get revenge or make the moment about himself. Instead, he showed tremendous humility in restraining his fellow black men and their justifiable desire for retribution and in working to address the legitimate concerns of the white minority, even though they had previously treated black men with contempt and abuse. His total focus on how to best serve the newly democratic nation was similar to Lincoln's. In his autobiography, *Long Walk to Freedom,* Mandela writes, *No one is born hating another person because of the color of his skin, or his background, or his religion. People must learn to hate, and if they can learn to hate, they can be taught to love, for love comes more naturally to the human heart than its opposite.* When we think about a smiling baby in its mother's arms, we know that love does come to us naturally.

Although we may not intuitively think so, many of the most successful business leaders, like political leaders, were also quite humble. One of my favorite business books is called *Built to Last,* by James Collins and Jerry Porras. They conducted a six-year research project to examine eighteen of *The Best of the Best* companies that had formed prior to 1950 and were widely recognized and admired by customers and peers. IBM, General Electric, and Walt Disney are among the group. One myth they shatter is that great companies require a charismatic leader. In their words, *A charismatic visionary leader is absolutely not required for a visionary (i.e. Best of Best) company and, in fact, can be detrimental to a company's long-term prospects.*

In a follow-up book called *Good to Great,* Collins researches eleven "good" companies that transitioned into "great" ones and identifies a key attribute of the companies that he calls Level 5 Leadership. This leader is *an individual who blends extreme personal humility with intense professional will.* Not surprisingly, these words could equally apply to Gandhi, Lincoln, and Mandela. Collins states these leaders *channel their ego needs away from themselves and into the larger goal of building a great company... their ambition is first and foremost for the institution, not themselves.* He acknowledges that this research finding cuts against the grain of conventional wisdom, as we think that larger-than-life leaders are needed to transform companies. Even though we are drawn to charismatic leaders, there is ample evidence that shows this style does not always produce the best results. We can do better with humility.

One of the most successful business leaders of our time, also among the wealthiest, Warren Buffet of Berkshire Hathaway, has demonstrated this humility by continuing to live in the same small house he bought in 1958, and by pledging to donate 99% of his wealth to charity to help solve the world's most pressing needs. He and Bill Gates of Microsoft have recruited many of the world's wealthiest people to join them in pledging the majority of their wealth to charitable purposes via *The Giving Pledge.* Roger Sant, the co-founder of AES Corporation (one of the largest independent power producers in the world) is one of the many wealthy individuals who has taken this pledge. I had the privilege to work with Mr. Sant for years as he was an investor in a company I had co-founded. He was as kind and humble a person as you could ever meet and was always focused on our employees and mission as priorities, not the return on his investment. Even in business where we think that fierce competition is the only way to win, humility seems to lead to something greater.

What is it about humility that is so powerful while at the same time running counter to our intuition? The power of humility is that it treats others as equals and lets go of our expectations of them. We do not look to others to serve our needs, instead we seek to serve others. We are not driven by our ego to compete with others. We are not looking to get something. With humility, we look for the opportunity to work together toward something better. Humble leaders listen and learn from others in order to elevate everyone, including themselves, toward a greater purpose. That is its power. When our ego competes, like a lion in a jungle, there cannot be many winners. But with our ego out of the way, we can collaborate and create something greater than would be possible working primarily for our self-interests. This is what all the humble leaders discussed above had in common. On the surface, this seems so simple and obvious that it raises the next question.

If humility is so obvious and powerful, why don't we all practice it? It all comes down to our lack of self-awareness. We work to satisfy our ego desires instead of understanding what we really need is love and connection. We are just too wounded to recognize this. The elephant runs away from our inner pain and society baits our ego by preying on our fears and desires. So gaining this understanding is hard work. ***If love and connection is our most fundamental need, then trying to satisfy our ego to fill this need is our most fundamental problem.*** We look for self-gratification to ease our pain, in the form of self-righteousness, power, wealth, fame, and pleasure. But studies show that focusing on such things does not help us in the long run. In fact, it is more likely to increase our depression and anxiety. When our ego leads the way, it is like putting a bandage over an infected wound. This may temporarily hide the problem, but the bandage is no cure and the pain persists or worsens. We need the courage to get in there and do the painful work of cleaning it out. Only then can the healing begin.

Like gratitude, all religious and philosophical traditions consider humility a virtue. In Buddhism, humility is an intrinsic part of enlightenment. That is, when you reach an enlightened understanding, you become humble, as mentioned earlier. It's a natural outcome of our inner work. Lack of humility demonstrates that such work is still to be done. Christian teachings are equally clear with Jesus saying in the Gospel of Matthew *Blessed are the meek, for they will inherit the earth,* and *Those who exalt themselves will be humbled and those who humble themselves will be exalted.* Some of the greatest religious and spiritual teachers of our current day, such as Pope Francis, the Dalai Lama, and Thich Nhat Hanh, demonstrate this humility.

Gandhi speaks of the Hindu understanding of humility from his love of the *Bhagavad Gita* and his life of devoted service. He, like Mother Teresa, believes that humility must emerge along with other virtues. Gandhi claims, *Humility cannot be an observance by itself. For it does not lend itself to being practiced. It is however an indispensable test of ahimsa (non-harming).* In other words, humility reflects a state of mind that is attained on the road to God or enlightenment, as taught in Buddhism. The term *Islam* can be interpreted as meaning *surrender to God,* or *humility*. Showing humility before Allah and His will is asked of every Muslim. In Taoism, humility is regarded among three treasured virtues, along with compassion and frugality.

Chapter Summary

We are born as humble little infants, completely dependent on our parents for survival. We normally get all the love and nurturing that we need for a while. As Nelson Mandela said, *love comes naturally,* both to us and from us. Then as we grow we learn that the love we receive is conditioned upon our behavior. We find out for the first time that we can be *bad* and unworthy of love. This is a shock, as we need love to survive. When we learn that the world is no longer safe and secure, it changes everything.

This description may be hard for some to believe and no doubt few of us have specific memories of these early moments, but it does not make it any less true. This is the basis for all of our insecurities. If love and acceptance were never taken away, we would have no insecurities and no problems. In a word, we would still feel *safe.*

Once we feel insecure, we start to fight for what we need. We try to prove we are worthy of love by measuring up to expectations or showing we are better than others. We are encouraged to compete and prove we are better from our earliest days in school. This continues into our adult lives. With our wounded egos in the driver's seat fighting for love and attention, it is no wonder we have problems. This is a game of winners and losers. Look around. It's being played everywhere, in our personal relationships, in our institutions, even in some churches. Humility, which is the opposite of our ego game, is almost nowhere to be found.

Humility does not put its own desires before others. It does not bind others in any way, but instead sets them free. It is not out to see what it can get, but asks how it can serve others and what can we create together. It listens to others without a personal agenda.

It seeks to elevate others and join them toward a greater purpose. It knows we can always do better. It retains a healthy self-doubt instead of self-righteousness, and always seeks greater knowledge and understanding. Humility becomes possible when we gain awareness of our internal suffering, then develop the compassion and understanding needed to shift. While we should still try to recognize the signs of an overactive ego and rein it in when possible, the real transformation to humility comes from the inner work we discussed in previous chapters.

As we become more self-aware, we are able to see others with our new understanding. We know that outward shows of self-confidence and authority demonstrate underlying insecurities. We see that self-righteousness and a victim mentality always go together. If we are always right, we can never be responsible when things go wrong. It is always the other person's fault. Therefore, when those around us project anything other than humility, they demonstrate they still have work to do. We use this awareness not to judge others, as we all have work to do. It is more to help us discern who to befriend, work with, or follow. Our quest for self-realization and love is aided by like-minded friends and leaders. When we join ego-based friends, leaders, and creeds, we slow or stop our growth. In worse cases, we regress, and this is the greatest danger to us personally and to our society.

This chapter ends with a text exchange between Katlyn and a dear friend who was breaking into the music business and had just shared a new song with her. I am so thankful to Katlyn for one of the most beautiful examples of humility I have ever seen.

Katlyn: *Nobody with a heart can hear it and not be blown away, Nobody can hear ur life story and not be inspired. I can hardly comprehend the future u have ahead of u and how many lives your going to touch. I have never met anyone like you. Theres so much garbage in the media now. People need someone worth looking up to, a true role model with god given talent, great morals, humility, ambition, beauty, strength, perspective, someone who always tries to do the right thing, someone to inspire us and bring us hope. I know that person is u.*

Friend: *Thank you :)! You are incredible! You are so contagiously positive and relaxed and you have such a beautiful and huge huge heart and you leave a massive impact on anyone who's lucky enough to meet you or know you or call you their friend. I'm so lucky I get to call you mine you inspire me so much and push me to be better and explore things without even knowing you're doing it. You make this life and place a thousand times more beautiful.*

Katlyn: *Ha ur silly. I just say what im thinking but thanks for all the compliments!!!!!!*

Chapter 7

The Practice: LAUGH

Energy and persistence conquer all things.

—Ben Franklin

In previous chapters, we discussed principles to live by that could help us create a better life. The purpose of this chapter is to recommend how to put these principles into practice. The approach will be to evaluate the best practices that science, religion, and ancient wisdom have offered and recommend practical methods that may work for us. In order to respect individual differences in our life circumstances, the recommendations offered here are less prescriptive and more menu-based. The idea is to propose things we could try and see what works best for us individually. The precondition to this work is that we agree to take responsibility for our own happiness and well-being. This is not meant to minimize the injustices and pain we can experience from others. But we are not trying to change things we cannot control. However, with these practices we should be able to interact with others more skillfully, even in difficult circumstances.

What I recommend as a starting point is that we set an overall intention for our practice. If you were drawn to this book from a desire to relieve anxiety and experience more happiness and peace of mind, then this would perhaps be your overriding intention. If your main intention is to better serve God and someday get to heaven, or even to achieve enlightenment, hopefully the practices here can help you as well. Once our overall goal is set, more specific intentions that would help us achieve our goal would follow. Based on the previous chapters, I would offer that we could try to *LAUGH* more. That is, we could try to become a little more:

Loving
Accepting
Understanding
Grateful, and
Humble

This, of course, reflects the principles to live by that we've been discussing. They are supported by both science and religion, and the word *LAUGH* passes the first test for any practice, as it's simple and easy to remember. This does not, however, mean that it's easy to do. Hopefully, the practice we develop will be easy enough that it only requires a sustained effort to manifest the changes we desire in time. The other nice feature of *LAUGH* is that the word implies where we are headed. If you have ever encountered an enlightened soul or someone filled with the grace of God, their near constant smile and gentle laughter is what most distinguishes them. My mother was a beautiful example of this. Non-believers filled with these qualities would have the same joyfulness about them, as does my friend Bill Wetzel whom I mentioned in the first chapter. So learning to *LAUGH a little bit more* has both a symbolic and literal meaning. *LAUGH* also reminds us not to take ourselves too seriously, which is always a good thing. Finally, for those who are religiously motivated, you could use the word *LAUGHING* and practice the same principles *In the Name of God.*

In setting more specific intentions or principles to practice, one could argue for any number of virtues that are not presented here, and also argue for less. For example, if we were to set the intention to be *kind to ourselves and all others, at all times, without exception,* it would be clear how this could ultimately lead to happiness, enlightenment, or bring us closer to God, if only we were able to actually do it. Most of us have issues that keep us from making such quantum leaps that we need to understand and address. With that said, please feel free to set your own intentions and principles to live a better life. Or try the *LAUGH* principles and let go of whatever does not work for you. The key is that we have a simple and clear ***intention*** to guide our work and transformation. The practices we propose will hopefully work equally well for different intentions, so long as they are positive and life affirming in nature and involve only ourselves.

Once we have set a clear intention, we need to commit to a certain level of effort. We need both a desire to change and a willingness to work at it. Remember our discussion on how hard it is to retrain the elephant, which is the part of our mind that reacts based on our instincts and conditioning. Most of what the elephant thinks is automatic and hidden in our subconscious mind, so we literally don't know what is motivating us. Next, the people in our life and modern society are powerful influences that often run counter to the retraining we need. Lastly, deep inside we feel insecure or unsafe, so we either run from these feelings or go on the attack. The combination of these factors is what makes retraining our minds so difficult. So a consistent ***effort*** is required.

Fortunately, once we set a clear intention and commit to a reasonable level of effort, if our efforts are correctly applied, the change we want for ourselves is assured. In other words, it is our nature to be more loving, happy, and peaceful once we become aware of what limits us. The third key to change, then, after intention and effort, is ***awareness***. This is where our efforts should be directed. The teachings of the Masters and the work of science show us that awareness is what is needed to change our minds.

That is, once we become aware of unconscious thoughts and feelings that are the cause of our suffering, we change them, not by our will, but just by acting in our own self-interest. It's the same way we learn not to touch a hot stove-top. No one needs to tell us what to do once we see that it hurts. This is the basis of cognitive therapy and meditation as well. Just gaining awareness. It's that simple, but still not easy. [Note: Deep emotional wounds are one exception as they are very difficult to heal. In more serious cases, such as with trauma or child abuse, specialized therapeutic interventions are often needed to heal the mind and restore normal cognitive abilities. We'll cover this topic in more detail in the next chapter.]

Gaining sufficient awareness to bring about change is where modern science can assist religion and ancient wisdom. These traditions typically tell us what to do, but don't say much about how to get there. When we look at the teachings of Jesus to *love our neighbor as ourself* and not to judge others, the similar teachings in Islam, the Buddha's Eightfold Noble Path, the Eight Stages of Yoga, the Ten Commandments, and others, there is no shortage of instruction on *what to do*. If it were easy, though, we'd all be living in bliss. The Buddha perhaps gave the most complete direction on *how* to change our minds for the better, but modern science still has something to add. So our practice will focus more on how and why we change. It is up to us individually to decide what we are trying to do, or our intention.

In summary, our practice is to set a positive *intention*, commit to some reasonable level of *effort*, and then direct our efforts toward gaining *awareness* of what keeps us from meeting our intentions. Once we achieve this awareness, the change we desire is assured. In my experience, if we can't make the change we desire (such as becoming more accepting, for example) then we still don't understand what is limiting us. The proposed practice should help us see if this happens. The weekly model to guide our recommended practice and level of effort is outlined in the following table.

Morning Practice (5 Days)	MPJ - Meditation, Prayer, Journal	10-30 minutes
	IOUs - Intentions, Observations, Understandings	
Daytime Practice (5 Days)	AOKs – Acts of Kindness	~10 seconds each
	M&HN - Movement & Healthy Nutrition	20 minutes minimum
	SIP - Staying in the Present	
Evening Practice (5 Days)	W4s – What Went Well & Why	10-30 minutes
	IOUs - Intentions, Observations, Understandings	
	MPJ - Meditation, Prayer, Journal	
Day 6 Practice	MPJ Morning and Evening	
	Life Inventory, IOUs Review plus AOKs, SIP, and M&HN	30-60 minutes
Day 7 Practice	MPJ Morning and Evening	
	Rest and Recharge, plus AOKs, SIP, and M&HN	As much as practical

Let's go through the proposed practice model step-by-step. First, it assumes a weekly schedule, with 5 days of standard practice and a progress review each week on Day 6. For people working a standard Monday through Friday work or school week, Day 6 would normally be Saturday. The practice is focused on morning activities, with the preferred time immediately after we awaken, and evening activities, with a similar preferred time of immediately before we go to sleep. The last thing you may glean from the model is the recommended practice can be done in as little as 10 minutes in the morning, 20 minutes during the day, 10 minutes in the evening for 5 days a week, and about 30 minutes on Day 6. My experience is that this represents the minimal level of effort required. For many people, more may be better. I have found that 30-60 minutes in the morning, afternoon, and evening work well for me, both in terms of fitting into my life schedule and producing the desired results. Next we'll walk through each segment and describe what is intended.

Morning and Evening Practice Elements

<u>Meditation and Prayer</u>: We seek to start and end each day with meditation and prayer because this is where we look to connect with ourselves, our Spirits, and/or our God. So it's important that we try to minimize distractions. Some people can meditate and pray in any place and at any time. But for most of us, this is not possible once we get into our daily routines. Even monasteries, where monks often devote their entire lives to meditation and prayers, normally focus their prayer and meditation efforts at the start and end of the day. Since this is what the "experts" do, we could try that approach unless we have a reason to do otherwise. And if the idea of meditation or prayer is not appealing, we could think of this as a time for quiet *contemplation* and introspection.

Many reading this may already have meditation and prayer practices. For those initiating these practices or looking to enhance their existing practice, here are some thoughts that may be helpful. We could define prayer as connecting and communicating with a higher power, such as God or a Universal Spirit, both of which we may see as residing within ourselves. In general, for purposes of this practice, listening to God or Spirit and prayers of thanksgiving can be most helpful, and prayers that ask God or Spirit for specific things may work against our goals. That is, if we are praying for specific things other than those associated with our basic needs, we are setting hopes and expectations and to a degree, basing our happiness on whether our prayers are answered. This may work against us taking responsibility for our own happiness and accepting things the way they are. As my mother said, *sometimes the answer to our prayers is no.* There is no right or wrong here, just an attempt to point out a possible trap. Asking for God's help or protection is comforting for many, including me. It's praying for specific outcomes, particularly those that involve others or that we don't control, that may pose a concern with regards to our practice.

For example, my morning prayer when I wake up in a hurry is simply, *Thank you, thank you, thank you. Please help me, help me, help me.* It may sound too simple, but it works for me. I like to start each day with gratitude for another chance to live my life and experience this world. We get to start over each day, so no matter how bad yesterday may have been or how many mistakes we may have made, each morning we have a fresh start and a new opportunity to create something better. My *help me* phrase is an acknowledgement that there is a higher power, or for non-believers even a higher nature within ourselves. I invoke this power in my quest to *LAUGH* a little bit more, as we have been discussing. This is my way of asking for help in retraining my inner elephant. The other important point is, my *thank you-help me* prayer is all about me and the things I can control, so it supports my practice.

Regarding meditation, there is plenty of good instruction available, so we don't need to add much here. However, it may be helpful to remember that the overall intention of meditation for purposes of this practice is to observe our inner thoughts and feelings to develop self-awareness. To do this, at minimum we should be comfortable and free of distractions. Nothing else is required. The common technique is sitting comfortably, focusing attention on the breath, and gently observing thoughts that arise, then letting them go without judgment and returning to the breath. With consistent practice, our mind should become more focused and less scattered. The *Bhagavad Gita* says, *Whenever the mind wanders, restless in its search for satisfaction without, lead it within; train it to rest in the self.* With meditation, over time we can gain both new awareness and greater mind control.

By contrast, some meditation techniques are so detailed that we can lose track of what we're trying to do. So we should understand that meditation is primarily an observation technique that allows us to calm our mind and better understand our subconscious thoughts, feelings, and motivations. With this understanding, we can select or develop a meditation practice that works best for us. The only suggestion I would offer from personal experience is that it may help to meditate or pray with a slight smile. This aids us in relaxing and letting go of fear. And fear is what keeps us from seeing our pain. When we smile, we are also practicing where we're headed, as mentioned earlier when discussing the word *LAUGH*. In the end, prayer, meditation, and contemplation as used in this practice are about making an inner connection to slow down our thoughts and develop greater awareness of our subconscious mind, and the Universal Mind or mind of God if that applies to you. Once we gain awareness, the next step is journaling.

<u>Journaling</u>: In journaling we make an effort to write down our observations, thoughts, and feelings in the present moment. The process of writing them down provides a record and allows time to reflect and consider what goes on inside our minds. Over time, through review of our journal entries and introspection, we can gain insight into the causes of our unpleasant feelings. While journaling can be done any time thoughts or feelings arise, writing immediately after prayer and meditation can be effective because this is where we purposely make observations and often gain new awareness. I also keep a journal at my bedside because insights

sometime come to me at night from dreams or when I awaken and I don't want to forget them when I fall back asleep. Some people also experience deeper awareness and clarity while engaging in physical activities such as running, hiking, surfing, yoga, or dance. Having a journal available soon after to record thoughts, feelings, or insights that arise during these activities can be very helpful.

Intentions, Observations, Understandings: *IOUs* are the main output of our practice and are also written in our journal. The intentions listed in the journal are the ones we set at the beginning of our practice. Our daily intentions then, derive from our overall intentions. We could use one of the *LAUGH* principles each of the 5 days of the week. For example, Monday could be our *Love and Kindness* day, Tuesday, *Acceptance Day,* and so on. At minimum, on Monday, we could set the intention to *be a little more loving and kind.* If we know of a specific person (including ourselves) or issue that could benefit from a more loving approach, we might weave that into our Monday intention as well. With our daily intentions, then, we can bring aspects of our practice into real life situations. This is where we start to learn how to create our own happiness. The idea is simply to start out each day with a positive intention and write it down. Next we record any thoughts and feelings that come up during prayer and meditation. These are the "observations" we make that are the source of our ever expanding self-awareness. Over time, hopefully our growing awareness leads to deeper understanding.

In summary, morning meditation, prayer, and journaling help us grow in awareness and understanding of our negative thoughts and feelings that limit our happiness. These are normally in our subconscious, so we remain unaware of what is motivating us or causing our pain. For those that feel particularly depressed or anxious, professional help in the form of a therapist or counselor is the best option. There is no shame in this as we are all a product of our inherited genes, conditioning, and environment. It takes courage to recognize our limitations and seek help. I wish I had sought such help twenty years sooner. Regardless of what path we choose, the process of gaining awareness and understanding of the source of our pain is gradual and requires a consistent practice and safe environment. Reading a book like this and coming to some intellectual understanding is not enough. We need a dedicated practice to experience these truths and come to know them, as Buddha said. When blocks in awareness or understanding arise, this is where a friend, family member, teacher, or therapist can be very helpful.

Daytime Practice Elements

Acts of Kindness: Acts of Kindness (AOKs) are one of three practice elements suggested during the day. The morning practice elements help us identify thoughts and feelings that cause our anxiety so we can learn to change our mind. This is similar to cognitive therapy and might be thought of as identifying and healing our emotional wounds. The other approach to gaining more happiness and peace in our lives is creative. Setting a positive intention each day supports this process. Such practices help us learn to create the conditions for our own happiness and are often identified with positive psychology, as mentioned earlier. Both types of approaches are important. As the Buddha stated, *Abandon what is unskillful. Cultivate the good.* Therapy, for example, helps us abandon what is unskillful. Setting positive intentions and practicing AOKs, Staying in the Present (SIP), and the gratitude exercise, What Went Well & Why (W4), which we discuss below, are among the most powerful exercises that help us *cultivate the good* and learn to create our own happiness.

We previously discussed how transformative a simple generosity exercise was for me. This is where I wrote down the kind things I had done in the past year for myself and others. As I took the time to think about it, I was surprised by the number of things on the list. Like our blessings, we tend to take the kind things we do for granted, as though we should always be doing more (the glass half-empty perspective). But when we take the time to recognize our generosity, we come to realize that we know the experience of kindness and we must have this within us or we could not offer it. This then, is the first step in realizing that the love we seek is within us. We could not overstate the importance of this realization, because after survival and security, love and connection is our most important need. If the love we need is really inside of us, we are not as needy as we think and we can give this love to ourselves and others, and create the loving connections that we need instead of constantly looking for it from others.

Acts of Kindness have another power that is equally important. When we offer kindness to another, especially when it is unexpected, this can literally make a person's day. Using a little math, we can see the profound effect of this "investment." If we assume it takes 10 seconds to say something kind, and with that, you make the other person feel better for the rest of the day, let's say 8 hours, that is a huge return on investment. Based on time invested, if 10 seconds provides 8 hours (28,800 seconds) of better feelings, that is a whopping 2,880 times return on investment. This may sound silly, but it's not. The impact of kindness is real. I still remember a kind comment made by a teacher in seventh grade and another in high school. Their comments had a profound impact on my self-confidence and direction in life. In the terms discussed above, it was like I had won the lottery and they had no idea what they had done for me. And in each case, the kind words they spoke lasted only seconds. This is not a new concept as there are many books available on the power of kindness and generosity.

If we tried to imagine a world where we routinely encountered kindness, you could see how transformative this would be for everyone. It costs us nothing but an open heart and a little time. And with every act of kindness we not only boost others, but also help ourselves by proving we have kindness and love inside. Our problem is we think we need love like we need food, as though it is something we get outside of ourselves that we need to keep consuming. *But what we really need is to **feel love** because that makes us **feel connected** and not alone, and that helps us **feel safe**.* With Acts of Kindness, we take control of creating this *feeling of love and* *connection* instead of looking for it outside of ourselves. Then we learn that love and kindness is available to us all the time and just part of our nature.

As a practical matter, the types of AOKs that are easy and effective are a smile, a touch or a hug (when appropriate), a thank you, holding the door, saying hello and asking someone how they are, letting someone go in front of you, offering a compliment or recognition, *I admire the wonderful work you did,* or a request for help that shows respect, *I was wondering if you would help me.* The AOK options are limited only by our imagination. Volunteering and charity are other forms of kindness that show us we have something worth giving and demonstrate we are valued by others. In the end, acts of love and kindness are not just powerful for what they give to others, but because they show us our higher nature and demonstrate our creative ability to fill our need for a loving connection.

Again, as Nelson Mandela said, *love comes naturally.* That is, we not only have an unruly and self-centered elephant inside us, but also the cutest little puppy dog that wants to wag its tail and jump on others to smother them with kisses. We never lose that aspect of our inner child, we just lose sight of it. It is no exaggeration then to say that *giving love and kindness to others can completely satisfy our need to feel love.* The child inside us that came into this world dependent on our parents for love does not believe this, but it turns out to be true nonetheless. We just need to do some healing and practice kindness before we can see it.

<u>Movement and Healthy Nutrition</u>: Ancient teachings and modern science both tell us that the health of our mind and body are inseparable. Therefore, we should not ignore our body if we want to change our mind and lives for the better. At minimum, we greatly benefit from healthy nutrition and regular movement each day. Being sedentary for most of the day, which is common in modern society, is quite detrimental to our physical health. By comparison, walking just 20 minutes a day has been shown to have a profound positive impact on health, adding years to our life by

dramatically cutting most major health risks. We should target at least 20 minutes of movement a day, such as a walk, run, or bike to and from work or school, or a similar exercise in the morning, at lunch time, or in the evening. It also helps to walk or use stairs whenever we have a choice. Practices that build strength, balance, and flexibility, such as dance, the martial arts, and yoga, can also be very beneficial. Of course, more extended and vigorous exercise can be even better for our health, especially when we are younger. Lastly, if you smoke, the most important thing you could do for your health is to stop.

Healthy nutrition comes from natural, whole foods, with limited processing. We should eat a balanced diet with fruits, vegetables, lean proteins, nuts, beans, and grains, and minimize consumption of sugars and unhealthy fats. The easiest way to change our eating habits is to buy healthy food. When junk food is around, it can be too hard to resist. It's also best to buy organic and non-GMO foods when possible. Organic foods have more of the nutrients we need and no dangerous chemicals like pesticides. And there's growing research on the dangers of GMO foods. One practice to help improve our nutrition is food journaling, where we record what we eat each day, along with the amount and type of calories we consume, to compare against a healthy diet plan. My experience is that food journaling for just two weeks changed my diet forever and helped me reach a healthy weight and sustain it. This reinforces that awareness and understanding is what we most need to make positive changes.

There is a fascinating book called *The Blue Zones* by Dan Buettner that examines five areas of the world where people live the longest—in Japan, Greece, Italy, the US, and Costa Rica. By researching behaviors in these areas, he developed a list of nine important lessons for living longer and better lives. Regular movement and a healthy diet are principal among them, as are other aspects of our recommended practice, such as meditation and prayer. My movement practice is to run or walk for 30 to 60 minutes each day on wooded trails, combined with 10 to 20 minutes of strength and flexibility exercises at home. This keeps me feeling strong and energized in my late 50's, and it's a routine I could perform most anywhere and continue for the rest of my life. For purposes of our practice, then, we recommend movement and healthy nutrition every day in a manner best suited to your lifestyle and tastes.

Staying in the Present: Life can only be lived in the present moment. There are no "do-overs." All of our power to create a better life is also in the present moment. So the vast majority of our time should be spent here in the present. When we dwell on the past or the future, we waste our energy on things we cannot change or control. Staying in the present does take effort, however. Our meditation practice helps us see where our mind constantly wanders and teaches us to gently bring it back to the present. When we bring this same focus on the present moment to our daily life, we notice that life becomes so much richer.

When we are fully present for our friends and family, for example, listening to them with our full attention, they will see and feel the difference. The quality of our relationships improves. When we eat our meals in the same way, the experience becomes much more enjoyable. We begin to feel a depth and beauty in life that we had previously missed. This truth is intuitive for us, but hard to put into practice. Sometimes using a little mantra as a reminder can be helpful. We could repeat a mantra such as *present moment or PM* to remind us of this during our day.

Our anxieties are nearly always about the past and the future. It is best to accept the past and learn from it, but not dwell there. And the future is mostly out of our control, so while planning for the future is appropriate, obsessing over it is not. It is good to work toward a future goal or destination, but even more important not to miss life's journey, because as a good friend once told me, *the journey is our life.* Anytime we are in the *present moment* and *feeling love,* which is what gratitude and kindness help us feel, we have attained the best that life can offer. Most of us have experienced this at times as a peaceful mind, light heart, joyfulness, or laughter.

We tend to dwell on things we want in the future and think we need so much more to be happy, but happiness is really more about finding feelings of love, joy, peace, and acceptance in the present moment.

Staying in the present and creating the feeling of love, then, is the key to our happiness. It is also within our own power once we have obtained the emotional healing we need. After survival and security, nothing else matters more. And it's something we can achieve with practice. Meditation helps us learn to control our minds and focus on the present. We also need to feel safe, which may require changes in our environment. Then we must learn to accept ourselves and our world, which again takes effort, but is possible with greater self-awareness and understanding. Once we feel safe and can accept the past, along with uncertainty about the future, we can live in the present and focus on kindness and gratitude, thereby creating our own happiness and well-being.

Evening Practice

What Went Well & Why: In the evening, the suggested practice is to repeat the meditation, prayer, and journaling we did in the morning just before bedtime, adding in the What Went Well & Why (W4) exercise mentioned earlier. The W4 practice is to write down things that went well each day and why. Acknowledging why they went well is important as it makes us aware of good people or things responsible for our blessings. Further reflection on our blessings shows us our creative power in bringing those good things into our lives. The number of blessings we write may not be critical, only that we recognize our blessings each day. When we add in "why" a blessing occurred, we should give consideration to our own efforts in creating the relationships or other conditions that are responsible. We may also find that our own Acts of Kindness mentioned earlier bounce back to us in ways that make us feel grateful. That is, we end up writing about our AOKs and the response of others as a blessing, showing us directly our power to create our own happiness.

Of course, the highest form of this practice is to feel gratitude throughout our day for our life, the air we breathe, our health, family, friends, home, food, and freedom from danger, as so much of humanity cannot even meet their basic survival and security needs. It is easy to take our blessings for granted, as modern society constantly tempts us with things that we don't need. We could also hold the intention to practice kindness at all times to the best of our abilities. When we consistently practice kindness and gratitude, we exercise our abilities to give and receive love. This shows us that we have the power to create the *feeling of love and connection,* which is what we most need.

Day 6 Practice

Life Inventory, IOUs Review: On the sixth day, which for many will be Saturday, the recommended practice is to take a *Life Inventory* that we'll describe below, and also to review the IOUs for the past week to see if there are new insights or understandings we can gain. We recommend practicing AOKs and Movement & Healthy Nutrition on Day 6 as well. The overriding goal of our practice is to set our intentions and over time to gently gain awareness and understanding of what is limiting us from meeting them. At the same time, we seek to build awareness of our power to create our own happiness and well-being.

The *Life Inventory* is a regular process of looking at our lives and asking ourselves some bigger questions, such as, *Who or what are my priorities and why? What was I expecting and why? What do I need to be happy? Where does my energy go and why? Where am I and what do I need right now?* The answers to these questions may not change each week, but over time they could change quite a bit. So regularly bringing such questions to mind is an important part of the practice. As with intentions, one could come up with any number of important life questions beyond what I have listed, so how we look at and review our lives is up to us individually to decide. As an example, however, we'll review these five questions to see how the Life Inventory might work.

Who or what are my priorities and why? As priorities, we might list our immediate family, closest friends, work or career, school and academic achievements, hobbies, our health, serving God and others, and our personal or spiritual development. The order of our priorities may also be helpful to think about, as in when our time is limited, what comes first? This is where we start to answer the question of "why" something is a priority and examine our purpose for living discussed at the beginning of the book. Our current priorities may not reflect our true nature, as many of our choices in life were likely based on trying to meet the expectations of others in order to gain the love and acceptance we crave. As a result, some of us are not satisfied with our careers or relationships, for example, and have yet to discover our real passion in life. So this question invites us to consider the fullest expression of who we are as individuals and to change our priorities or undertake new activities in order to discover our true passion(s) in life.

Once we review our current priorities and why, then acknowledge that these can change, there is one other rule I apply that may be helpful. When we need to keep something in mind, it should stay simple, as there's a limit to how much the mind can hold while still functioning with daily tasks. So I use the *five-finger-rule.* If there are more items than I can put on the fingers of one hand, then I reduce them down to only the five most important. The *LAUGH* principles follow this rule. For my life inventory, then, my regular priorities are immediate family, close friends, personal development, health, and service. More specific priorities can come up from time to time as well.

What was I expecting and why? What do I need to be happy? We covered this in detail in a previous chapter when we spoke about the glass being half-empty or half-full. In general, the idea is that we may need a lot less than we think to be happy. Our unmet expectations can be a major source of our unhappiness. Another key point is we often set hopes and expectations around things we cannot control; for example, our success in attaining career goals, which are only partly within our control. Since we can only control ourselves, expectations around things that depend upon others can lead to suffering. The goal in answering these questions is to bring awareness. Then we let our awareness and understanding bring about any changes needed in their own time.

Where does my energy go and why? Where am I (physically and mentally) and what do I need right now? We talked about how the need for distraction can be a defense mechanism that keeps us from facing our inner pain. When we look at where we spend our time and mental energy, we can evaluate if this is productive in terms of achieving our intentions. How is this working out for us? Are the things we spend our time on bringing us happiness and well being, or do they distract us, medicate away our pain, entertain our ego, and keep us stuck where we are? Another trap is thinking there is always more we "should be doing," when what we may need is to slow down and ask what we need right now. We may need to go for a long walk or take a nap, for example. Insight and wisdom does not easily flow to the mind that is constantly busy or stressed. Again, the idea here is just to ask the questions and bring awareness, not to judge ourselves. Our increased awareness and understanding will lead to positive change by itself when we're ready. This is the only way we can make sustainable changes.

When we try to change our negative thoughts or habits using our willpower alone, we most often fail. The first reason is that we don't understand our underlying motivations, which are the things we really need to change. The next reason is because our mind focuses on the very thing that we are trying *not* to do, giving it more energy and power. Just try to not think about a word. Your mind will keep checking in to see how you are doing, and you will therefore think of that word far more than if you had never tried. Dieting is another good example, the more we think about the foods we are not supposed to eat, the more we crave them. There's an old saying, *what we resist persists.* And as mentioned earlier, the elephant will most always win a battle of wills with the rider. It takes a well-directed and persistent effort toward greater awareness to retrain it.

Alternatively, when we seek to change using our new awareness and understanding, our actions can be done out of self-love as opposed to self-loathing. If we choose thoughts and actions that are positive, the negative ones fall away of their own accord in their own time. The idea that *when we know better, we do better* is true. Like the example of learning not to touch the hot stovetop; once we know it hurts, it's automatic to refrain. If we are losing weight or exercising vigorously because we dislike our bodies, for example, we are not likely to have long-term success, because we are constantly reminding ourselves that we are not good enough. If we eat healthier food and go for a walk everyday because we learn that it tastes good and feels good, and we want to be good to ourselves, then the change becomes self-sustaining, especially with this type of practice where we regularly focus on loving ourselves a little more.

In summary, the Day 6 Life Inventory and IOU Review is about assessing where we are each week in the hopes of increasing our self-awareness and understanding. Morning and evening meditation and prayer is always beneficial. Like the rest of our practice, we write our Day 6 observations in our journal. This is the point where a good friend to talk with can be very helpful, particularly a friend who is also going through this practice or something similar. The changes we seek are not easy to make and in general the influences we encounter daily are not supportive. It's common for people seeking positive changes to join groups that provide emotional support and helpful insights. Examples are churches or spiritual communities, exercise groups such as running clubs, weight loss groups, and even book clubs. For us, the support of a single good friend or family member who is empathetic could be extremely helpful.

Day 7 Practice

Rest and Recharge: The last practice day of the week, Day 7, is reserved for resting and recharging. As the name implies, this is about taking a break, slowing down, and doing something that is restorative and uplifting. The types of activities included should be intuitive for most of us, but obvious examples are church services, outings in nature, long naps, reading a book, and participation in the arts such as music, dance, and museums. Family gatherings, trips, and meals, which were a staple of my childhood on Sunday after church, can also be quite uplifting. The point is to take a break from our normal routines, recharge our batteries, and allow time for our new self-awareness to sink in. Again, morning and evening meditation and prayer is helpful and practicing AOKs, SIP, and M&HN is recommended everyday.

General Practice Reminders: Now that we have reviewed the elements of our proposed Practice, there are two important reminders. First, we all need a practice that works for us, with the time and energy we have available, and with our individual intentions for a better life. The invitation here is to try this proposed Practice or something different to find out what works best for you. As long as we start with positive intentions to work on ourselves, and we commit some level of consistent effort toward gaining self-awareness and understanding, then the better life we desire is not only possible, but probable.

The second reminder is this Practice is like meditation itself; it sounds easy but can be difficult at first. The key is to not judge ourselves when we miss days or certain practice elements like journaling. We can always come back to it and start again. Even one or two days a week is better than nothing. Awareness and understanding is cumulative, like walking on a long journey. If in some weeks we don't walk far, it's okay. Every step counts and once we have started on this path, it is less likely we would regress. Hopefully, as we gain more experience with the Practice, it will become more natural and easy to do and we'll come to realize that we feel better on days we do it.

My experience is that the Practice always gives more than it takes. That is, the benefit is much greater than the time it costs, like acts of kindness. This should not surprise us, as the Practice is an act of kindness toward ourselves. When I wake with my Practice, my day starts out much better and normally stays that way. Days when I miss parts of my Practice, especially the morning, are usually worse. The Practice is like exercise in that regard. When exercise is done correctly, the benefits in daily energy and positive feelings far exceed the time and energy cost of the exercise itself. But we have to experience this aspect of our Practice to come to know it. Once we do, we no longer have to struggle to find the time, energy, or motivation to practice. We do it out of self-love.

A limited discussion of some practical applications of the *LAUGH* principles is provided in the Appendix, which offers thoughts on relationships, conflict, parenting, who and what to follow, and teaching.

Chapter Summary

In previous chapters, we discussed principles to live by that could help us create a better life. The purpose of this chapter is to recommend how to put these principles into practice. The key elements of our practice are positive *intentions* combined with a consistent level of *effort* focused toward gaining *awareness* of what keeps us from meeting our intentions. Ancient wisdom, science, and our experience all tell us that once we achieve greater awareness and understanding of our negative thoughts and feelings, the positive change we desire is not only possible, but likely.

We have proposed a practice model that helps us identify our limiting thoughts and feelings through regular meditation, prayer, and journaling. The model should work equally well for any positive intentions that are focused on ourselves. We recommend using the *LAUGH* intentions to become more loving, accepting, understanding, grateful, and humble, as these are fundamental to leading a better life. We also recommend generic practice elements that help us learn to create our own happiness and well-being, such as acts of kindness, gratitude exercises, staying in the present, regular movement, and healthy nutrition. It is usually helpful to have a family member, friend, counselor, or therapist to support us as we try to make positive changes in our lives. Of course, we should also feel free to adapt this practice model to what suits us best.

In the end, the understanding of how to best live our lives cannot be given to us, but only learned by our own journey. The recommended practice presented in this chapter is one approach, but there are as many possible variations as there are individuals. So, we need to keep our positive intentions in mind and strive to gain greater awareness and understanding in a manner best suited to who and where we are in life. Our minds want this "wisdom" right away, but there is no short cut. Like most everything else in life worth having, we need to devote our time and focused efforts to reap the benefits.

This chapter ends with two more tributes to Katlyn. This is from a family member:

We all sat around a fire after dinner and told ridiculous stories to each other, and when Jess and I left for home at the end of the night, I remember telling her 'Katlyn is the nicest person I've ever met; easily the nicest person in your family. There's no way she's actually that nice in real life. She has to have some kind of alter ego where she robs banks, and plots to blow up the moon with a laser cannon like a James Bond villain.' But no, you were actually that nice and that positive, and you were always very fun to hang out with when I was fortunate enough to spend time with you.

This one is from a fellow lifeguard:

You get to see your coworkers in certain lights that most others don't. I'll always be grateful for those windows into you and your life and what I learned from you. Along with all the ridiculous blunt filter-less (but totally polite) comments and endless laughs along the way.... You were a kind and beautiful person Katlyn. And an integral part to the amazing, close-knit beach community that we became a part of summer after summer; one that will never be the same without you. You're missed more than you'll ever know polite girl.

Chapter 8

For the Love of Katlyn

Cause love is the answer. It's the answer to the questions in your mind.

—Aloe Blacc

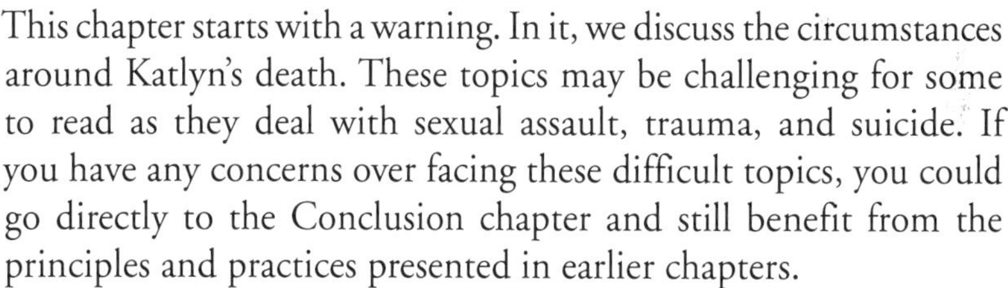

This chapter starts with a warning. In it, we discuss the circumstances around Katlyn's death. These topics may be challenging for some to read as they deal with sexual assault, trauma, and suicide. If you have any concerns over facing these difficult topics, you could go directly to the Conclusion chapter and still benefit from the principles and practices presented in earlier chapters.

This book began with my intention to honor Katlyn's life and learn from her suicide so that others might get the emotional healing they need to avoid such suffering and tragedy. It should be clear from the previous chapters that Katlyn was a beautiful and kind-hearted soul who had positively impacted many lives. When someone like Katlyn decides to leave this world, it is important to ask why. Just weeks before her suicide, Katlyn told me of her dream to work at a native seal rescue center in Hawaii to help restore their dwindling population, and then work together with the seals and people who are suffering to help bring emotional healing to herself and others.

This statement was another clear acknowledgment that Katlyn was fully aware of her own emotional wounds and need for healing. So this chapter honors Katlyn's dream to help bring healing to herself and others. It provides my limited understanding of what happened to bring Katlyn to the point of suicide, why she didn't get the help she needed, and what could have been done differently to prevent it. Because the details around Katlyn's life and even her last few months could fill another entire book, I necessarily have to be brief and focus on only the most important factors in her life that may have led to her choice, as best I can understand them, and what they can teach us.

College Years

Katlyn's life seemed to improve initially when she moved to college. She loved the ocean and marine mammals and dreamed of becoming an animal trainer. I remember when she was in high school and *Shark Week* came on TV, she would be giddy with excitement. We looked for colleges with marine science programs and took a road trip together to Florida to tour several of them. When we arrived at Eckerd College in St. Petersburg, she immediately fell in love. It was a small school, right on the water, with a large white sand beach. It reminded her of her high school as it was small enough that she wouldn't feel lost. They offered her a generous scholarship and we were both filled with hope and excitement as she started the next phase of her life.

Although college started out well for Katlyn, with a good roommate and advisor, and many new friends, she eventually experienced problems. She had confrontations with different people that ended with strained relationships. She also experienced conflicts with classmates during group projects. Katlyn always maintained that the conflicts were the other person's fault, as they were being self-centered and inconsiderate. While this may have been true, I had witnessed her tendency to emotionally react to injustice many times. Her behavior pattern showed that she needed to learn to control her emotions and develop sufficient human relation skills to constructively work through such issues.

I tried to discuss this with her gently, but made little progress as she seemed threatened by my comments and would not acknowledge her contribution to the problem. Even though Katlyn had broken out of her victim mentality with me, she still reverted back to this with others and seemed to take every offense personally. We had worked together to build trust, but with others it seemed that she didn't feel safe. Her hypersensitivity to personal injustice combined with her tendency toward emotional responses limited her ability to work through the inevitable challenges of human relationships. And her fear in facing her own emotional wounds kept her from the help she needed to understand and heal them. Though I could see this clearly, I could not find a way to help her.

Her college struggles reached a crisis stage at two different times. In her second year, near the end of the fall term, Katlyn collapsed unconscious while walking to a class. She was transported by ambulance to a local hospital where she was treated and released. Katlyn called to tell me that she had fainted due to extreme anxiety over school. She said she had been struggling with certain classes and had not been eating or sleeping much. She finished up her final exams in the next few days and came home for winter break. Katlyn was exhausted at the time so I gave her some time to recover before discussing the problem with her.

When we talked, I wanted Katlyn to get help to deal with the stress of school before she returned. She then told me she had been to the school counseling office for depression months earlier and had been put on antidepressant medication. She did not receive any therapy or counseling, just the medication. When I researched her medication, I was surprised to learn that it had a serious warning for increased risk of suicide among people under twenty-five years of age. This alarmed me and I objected to her taking the medication, telling her that any added risk of suicide was unacceptable to me. I thought she needed professional help in the form of therapy. She argued with me on this, telling me that she needed the medication to get out of bed in the morning and did not want to go to therapy. I told her that I didn't want her to get out of bed unless she was getting help for her anxiety and depression, and also said the drugs would not help cure her real problems.

I decided to take her out of school until she got the help she needed, as she could not attend without my financial support. When I told her this she again argued with me passionately, stating this would ruin her life. So I was faced with the dilemma of trying to decide what was best for her, knowing she was still resisting the help she needed, but also knowing how much she needed my love and support right now. After a long discussion, she agreed to get counseling at school and speak with me regularly on the phone, as well as incorporate other changes into her routine to help with her anxiety, such as daily exercise and healthy eating. We wrote down her commitments and with those promises, I agreed to let her return to school. She did not immediately get off the antidepressant medication, but she agreed this was the long-term goal as she got help for her anxiety and depression.

Later that school term Katlyn said she was feeling better and decided she no longer needed to see the school counselor since it was not helping her much anyway. I made it clear that I did not agree with her decision, as it was obvious to me that she still had not addressed her underlying emotional problems. And she was still taking the antidepressants. But there was not much I could do to force her without causing another major crisis. Since she was continuing to resist getting help, I reasoned that she would just have to learn things the hard way as I had done for so many years. So I resolved to continue to love and support her as best as I could.

Almost two years later, Katlyn had another serious crisis months before graduation when she became extremely upset because some girlfriends were mean to her. When Katlyn told her boyfriend about the incident, she told him she wanted to cut the girlfriends out of her life, but he suggested she should try to work it out with them. This made her feel like both her girlfriends and boyfriend had turned against her. She reacted badly and broke up with her boyfriend on the spot. After he left her apartment, Katlyn took some ibuprofen pills and ran out the door. Fearing the worst, her roommate went after Katlyn and called 911. They found Katlyn and got her to a hospital emergency room where she was evaluated overnight. She had taken few enough of the pills that there were no adverse physical effects. However, based on what appeared to be a suicide attempt, they assigned Katlyn to a psychiatric facility for a couple days so she could be evaluated.

I arrived to see her the day she was released from the facility and again tried my best to discuss what had happened and what we should do about it. Her boyfriend was back with her at the time and they both tried to downplay the incident as though it was just a momentary cry for help and that she didn't really intend to harm herself. This was not very comforting to me, as once again I saw a wounded little girl who was not capable of handling the difficult issues that inevitably arose in her life. I struggled to decide if it was safe to leave her in school, even though she would graduate in less than two months. The only good option seemed to be to let her finish school, as she begged me to trust her enough to do this. So we made a pact that she would do the things she needed to take care of herself and also agreed to talk daily, though her agreements to stay in touch with me never seemed to last very long. I would soon end up sending emails and leaving voice messages that were not returned.

Work Experience

After graduation, Katlyn took a job as an intern at one of the larger marine aquariums in Florida where her pattern of relationship issues reappeared, both at work and with her roommates. She had good explanations for the problems she encountered and I believed there was much truth in the way she viewed others and the injustices she experienced. However, it also appeared that Katlyn was still hypersensitive to perceived injustices and did not have the skills to constructively deal with these situations. There seemed to be little point in me discussing these problems with her, as she would just shut down when I suggested that she might learn to deal with these situations better. Over time, Katlyn had frustrated me in my attempts to help her, to the point where I had to accept that she would need to learn things by herself. At least her latest problems did not appear to be as serious and emotional as those she experienced in college.

Katlyn soon moved on to another marine mammal intern job in Florida. But these jobs did not pay well and she was diligently looking for an entry-level animal trainer job. One such opportunity soon came up in Hawaii, and to her surprise, she was offered the job. Katlyn immediately asked for my help in moving to Hawaii so she could accept the offer. I asked her where she would live and how she could possibly afford the living expenses, but she had spoken extensively with her prospective employer and seemed to have good answers to all of my questions. She also told me that her college boyfriend was going to try to get a job there and join her, which he confirmed when I spoke to him. However, this still presented another difficult decision for me, as Hawaii was a 13-hour flight from where I lived on the east coast and she had no friends out there. Working as a trainer at a dolphin facility was Katlyn's "dream job," and as was her way, she begged me to support her. Despite my reservations, and the difficulty and cost of moving her out there, I could not say no.

When I think back now about Katlyn's work and living experiences, it seems like she was happy and successful about half the time. She worked as an intern at the Clearwater Aquarium for three years during college and she always loved it there, and they loved her back. The same was true of her experience as a lifeguard at the local town beach, which was her summer job throughout college. Everyone there was very close. She loved the work and her co-workers remained close friends. She had a similar experience with some of her roommates and at one of her restaurant jobs, where she developed long-term loving relationships. These experiences, along with the few close friends she had maintained, gave me hope that Katlyn would find her way in time, even though the type of problems I mentioned above would routinely surface in new living environments. Unfortunately, her new job in Hawaii fell into the category of experiences that did not go well for her.

Hawaii

Within a couple weeks of starting her new job in Hawaii, Katlyn was put on notice that she did not have the animal trainer qualifications she needed and that she was in danger of being terminated. Her employer's position was that she had misrepresented her qualifications and experience when she applied for the job. Katlyn's viewpoint was that her boss had fabricated this charge since her boss' boyfriend, who also worked there, had taken a keen interest in Katlyn and began to flirt with her. Katlyn believed that her boss just wanted to get rid of her because of the perceived threat Katlyn posed to her boss' relationship, though Katlyn said she had tried to avoid the boyfriend. While it was impossible to know the real truth of this situation, I could believe that Katlyn may have exaggerated her qualifications to get the job, and could also believe that her boss was jealous of her. Katlyn was attractive, charming, and extremely fun to be around, and I know that some guys found her irresistible. Regardless of how and why it happened, two weeks later Katlyn was unemployed.

We now had another mini-crisis and more decisions to make together. Katlyn wanted a chance to stay in Hawaii and find another job. She said the people there were so friendly and treated her like family (with the exception of the employer who let her go, of course). After some discussion, I agreed to support her for a couple more months to see if she could work things out. At the time, there was still hope that Katlyn's boyfriend would move there and her car was still in transit, shipping from Florida. So it was not the right time to pull the plug on her dream. Within a few weeks, she had found a couple of new jobs, one with a company that provided ocean diving trips, wild dolphin swims, and sunset cruises along the coast, and another waiting tables at a restaurant located on the water.

When Katlyn learned that her boyfriend could not find a job in Hawaii and would not be moving, she seemed to go through some depression, questioning if she had done the right thing. We talked about it, but she was determined to stay. I visited her there in

August of 2013, about five months after she arrived, and it seemed like something was not right with her. She had a new boyfriend who was very sweet and loving to her, and two new places to work where the people seemed to care for her, but she was also anxious, like she was hiding something from me. I brought Katlyn her dog Teddy, as it took months to get approval to bring him to Hawaii. This lifted her spirits, like the reuniting of a mother and child. Teddy was so excited when he saw her and I felt relieved that she would have his love and support again.

After I returned home, we talked fairly regularly and she kept me posted on work and her relationships. Katlyn was just barely making enough money to survive, so she was constantly looking for a better job. When we visited her again in May of 2014, she had received a new job offer at one of the larger dive companies on the island where she would be able to qualify as a dive master and have better career opportunities. She also found a big, beautiful house to live in near work that she would share with three other roommates. After meeting the supervisor at her new job and the older woman that leased Katlyn a room in the new house, I came away once again hopeful that Katlyn had found great people to work and live with and was making her way. She seemed to be happier and genuinely excited.

But within three to four months, both her new job and living situation became untenable. At work, the older woman that had hired her left the company, and she got a new, young, female boss. Then she became close to a young male dive master that some other girls at work liked. Katlyn said that once he took an interest in her, the other girls turned against her and started to make up things about her neglecting her work duties. The new boss was friends with the other girls and so was not on Katlyn's side. I found this believable, as Katlyn had no trouble getting along when people were reasonable to her and was always extremely conscientious about her work. She may have been overly sensitive to the situation, as in the past, but her new job became very uncomfortable for her in spite of her efforts to be an exemplary employee.

Around the same time, the older woman who rented Katlyn the room had to travel back to California to care for her sick parent. A new male tenant who was a friend of the other two young women living in the house moved in. The three of them had a serious drug habit that Katlyn had no interest in joining, so she kept to herself. Their near constant partying led to friction between Katlyn and them, which came to a head when they damaged some furniture in the house. Katlyn made sure the landlord knew she did not cause the damage, and when her roommates found out that she had told the landlord, they turned against her. Katlyn said they became increasingly threatening to her and started to put her little dog outside of the fenced area while she was at work as a way to get back at her.

As a result, Katlyn felt unsafe in her house and searched hard for another place to live. She was not sleeping much due to all the stress at work and at home, and had come down with serious stomach pains that made it difficult for her to eat. She made an appointment to see a doctor, and near the end of September had reached her limit when she accidently backed her car into another. She called me in tears that morning and pleaded for my help. We spent a good deal of time talking about her problems and making a list of steps she could take to work her way through them. Later that same day I was thinking of getting on a plane to go help her when she called me again and said she needed to come home. She had met with a doctor that afternoon who told her that she didn't have the support system in Hawaii that she needed to succeed and the best thing she could do right now was get home and try to recover from the extreme stress she was feeling. So I gladly got her a plane ticket and she was home three days later.

Home Again

I remember the relief I felt when I picked up Katlyn at the airport. I had spent so much energy worrying about her. I thought, at least now she was home and would be safe. Katlyn looked exhausted and was still pretty upset. She vented about her mother, saying that when she pleaded with her mom for help in Hawaii, all her mother said was, *Just do whatever you want.* Katlyn went on to say that she knew I was the one who really loved her because I was the only one who visited her in Hawaii and the only one who was always there for her. It was strange to hear Katlyn talk that way, as she rarely said anything bad about her mom, even though I knew their relationship was strained. Still, I was pleased that she could see how much I cared for her. I would tell her all the time, *You know, I would do anything for you,* and I felt like she now believed it.

For the first month she was home, Katlyn seemed to be doing much better. She began working out regularly, eating better, going out with old and new friends, and planning for her return to Hawaii. She wrote me the following note in a birthday card just days after returning:

Happy Birthday Daddy! I'm so thankful to call you my Dad and I'm so happy to be home to spend the holidays. I feel like every year since I started college we have gotten closer and made up for lost time. You're the most fun Dad to be around EVER! And you always take care of me when I need you. Love, Katlyn

P.S. You love me the most

My wife and I noted Katlyn's improving attitude and helped her update her resume and write a cover letter for a job she wanted to apply for when she returned to Hawaii. My wife wrote this note in her journal regarding our experience in helping Katlyn at the time:

I told her I was tearing up at the thought of her leaving so soon (to return to Hawaii). *I told her that I loved her and that I just wanted her to be happy. She said that was so sweet I might make her cry. I also told her that her Dad loved her so much that he would do anything for her. She said, 'I know. You came and visited me twice in Hawaii.' She later sent me a text thanking me for helping her and for being so good to her Teddy. She said she really appreciated that and it meant a lot to her. During this time she also said that if her Dad and I got married again, she would come this time.*

The first sign that something was wrong with Katlyn came in early November after we had finished with her resume and application letter for the job in Hawaii at the seal rescue center mentioned earlier. She said she wanted to go back to Hawaii soon and had some good friends she could live with until she found a permanent place. But she had only been home about a month and did not yet have the job. I also thought the stress and anxiety that had caused her to leave Hawaii could not have fully healed and told her that before she went back I wanted her to have a good job, a permanent place to live, and wanted to make sure she had gotten the healing she needed to feel strong again and succeed. When I said this she just shutdown and looked away. I didn't understand her reaction, so I gently said that we had to be able to talk about these things before I could agree to send her back. Then she got up and left. Her reaction was a big departure from the positive attitude I had seen for several weeks and it concerned me.

Over the next month, we continued to talk regularly and meet each other each week for dinner, but I could see Katlyn was getting depressed about being stuck at home. At different times she would mention not having a real job, or her own car, or even a sure path back to Hawaii. I understood that these things caused her stress, but didn't have a simple answer or solution. She was continuing to hang out with friends, work out, and take better care of herself, so at least I thought she was on the path back to physical health. Katlyn also started providing after school care for a sweet young girl several times a week and this seemed to bring some joy and meaning back into her life. The picture at the start of this chapter is that same young girl kissing Katlyn.

Days before Thanksgiving, we went out together to shop for new eyeglasses, with each of us helping pick out the glasses for the other. She seemed somewhat subdued at the time, but she had requested that we do this together and was still engaging as we shopped and tried on new glasses. Then I saw her at a family party the day after Thanksgiving and things had changed. She arrived with her older brother and was shutdown and quiet in a way I had never seen her around family. A number of family members asked why she was home again so soon, as she had recently been home for a week in early September. Katlyn had no answer and seemed embarrassed. I imagined she must have felt like a failure in front of them and started to worry more about her state of mind. As this was no place to talk, I just told her I wanted to get together soon.

The following Monday she called me quite sad and said that nothing ever seemed to work out for her. I saw this as my opening and gave her a long pep talk as I had many times before. I told her that several things in my life had also not worked out, but that when things went badly, I had learned to focus on my own health and strength so I could get through the hard times. I would also spend time with people I loved the most because those things mattered most in life. I reinforced that since she came back home, she had done just that, by taking better care of herself and working out to get stronger, and by spending time with her family and friends. I told her I was proud of her for doing these things and offered to get together with her and map out a plan to get back to Hawaii. We seemed to have good success creating such plans in the past and I was trying to give her some hope that she could once again create what she wanted with my help. She didn't talk much, but we agreed to get together the next day to work on a plan of action.

I texted her the next day (Tuesday):

What's the plan?

Katlyn responded, *I don't feel well*

I replied, *ok. Sorry. Maybe tomorrow. xo*

I called her on Wednesday and left her a voice message saying she really needed to call me so we could get together. I didn't hear from her, so I left another voice message, more strongly worded, requesting that she call. Katlyn then texted me, *Hey daddy was playing ping pong downstairs with* (my brother) *and mommy*

I responded, *jealous!*

She went on to text me about her friend who just had a baby girl and also texted me a picture of the mom and baby to which I responded, *Oh wow. Call me and tell me about it.*

She then called me and seemed pretty upbeat about the baby news. I once again suggested we get together the next day (Thursday), but she said she was watching the young girl after school and promised we could get together on Friday. That was the last time I spoke to Katlyn.

Unimaginable

The next day, December 4th, at around 2pm I received a screaming, barely intelligible phone call telling me to come to her mother's house right away. In the confusion, I thought the call was from Katlyn and that something awful had happened to her mom. I told her to call 911 and sped over there in tears because I surmised that her mother had done something to harm herself. This is what I told my wife as I left for their house. There are no words to express what I felt when I arrived there to instead see Katlyn lying on the ground with emergency medical technicians trying to revive her. I don't know how I lived through that moment. I just bent over, grasping onto my gut with both arms, crying out "NO!," "NO!," over and over. I wanted to die and give her life back to her. I remember a policewoman trying repeatedly to calm me down and telling me that if I didn't stop crying out in pain I would have to leave the scene.

We rode with Katlyn in the ambulance to the hospital where the medical team spent another hour trying to revive her without success. Immediately after the doctor suspended efforts to revive Katlyn, her mother climbed on top of her petite, dead body and began reciting bible verses, speaking in a guttural, gibberish voice ("tongues"), and pulling tubes out of Katlyn's mouth so she could breath into her mouth in an attempt to raise Katlyn from the dead. She continued doing this frantically for several minutes until I gently told her that Katlyn had made her decision to leave and if she were coming back to life, it would have already happened. Then she stopped and got off Katlyn's body. Witnessing this scene was very disturbing for me and the medical professionals in the room. It was unbelievable that Katlyn had taken her own life. Equally unbelievable was what her mother had just done in response. This turned out to be an omen for what was to follow.

The staff took us to a nearby waiting room while they summoned the medical examiner. There were seven of us together, as Katlyn's mother and I were joined by her church pastor and his wife, my wife, and one of my sons and his girlfriend. I then overheard Katlyn's mother nervously asked her pastor *if she should tell me what had happened to Katlyn*. I was shocked to hear her ask him for permission and immediately demanded that she tell me anything she knew about why this happened. Over the next several minutes, her mother informed us of the following facts related to Katlyn's suicide:

- When Katlyn was home in September (three months earlier), Katlyn told her mom that she had been raped in Hawaii. When I asked her mom why she didn't tell me about this, she said Katlyn didn't want her to tell me and she was just respecting Katlyn's wishes.
- Weeks prior to her suicide, her mother told Katlyn she should increase her antidepressant intake to double its prescription strength (20mg to 40mg) in order to better manage her depression. Her mom thought this would be helpful, although she did not discuss this with the prescribing doctor.
- The day before, her mother had stayed home from work after Katlyn told her that she was contemplating suicide. Her mother also thought this had been helpful, although she did not seek any medical support or outside advice, or inform me. Today she had gone back to work and left Katlyn home alone.

When I asked why she did not seek medical or other professional help for Katlyn's rape or thoughts of suicide, her mother stated in her defense that, *We broke off the shame,* referring to herself and her church group. Stunned by her response, I asked what this was. She said it was a prayer ritual. When I asked why this ritual was done, she described Katlyn's sexual history and how the only sex Katlyn had prior to her rape was with a man who she intended to marry, implying that this was morally acceptable. But after her rape, Katlyn had sex with other men she did not intend to marry, implying that she had become immoral, which supported her action to remove the shame from Katlyn.

That was all I could take. I was so upset and dumbfounded by her actions and remarks that I could not bear to hear anything more. Learning these factors surrounding Katlyn's suicide immediately after her death was shocking beyond words. I was an emotional wreck, not just for Katlyn's loss, but also because of the horrible things that preceded it. There was too much going on in my head to make any sense of it. All I knew for sure was that everything about Katlyn's suicide, and what her mother had done prior to it, seemed wrong. I struggled with the question of why her mother didn't tell me these things sooner, and why Katlyn didn't let me see her in the past few days. Though I still couldn't understand how Katlyn would have chosen this, my immediate feeling was that her suicide could and should have been prevented. With just one word from Katlyn or her mother, I would never have left Katlyn's side. By keeping all of this information from me until after Katlyn's death, her mother kept me from Katlyn in her greatest time of need. I could not imagine how she had failed to see the seriousness of Katlyn's situation and failed to tell me.

Search for Understanding

I barely got through the next day, and then only because my wife was able to coax me out of a chair or the bed. I did not want to go on with life. But she asked me to take one step at a time, and I slowly learned that this was possible. When we met as a family to talk about what had happened and plan services for Katlyn, I was still searching for understanding and asked her mother several more questions. When I asked why she didn't take Katlyn's thoughts of suicide more seriously, she shrugged her shoulders and gave no reply. When I mentioned that she had no right to increase Katlyn's depression medication without a doctor's approval, she said in her defense that she had routinely altered the dosage of her sick mother's medication in the past and therefore felt qualified.

Over the next several days, I continued to question why Katlyn didn't come to me for help, as she had made it clear to me that she understood how much I loved her. Something that happened in the hospital made me wonder if her mother had something to do with this. While we were waiting for the emergency room staff to admit Katlyn, her mother told me to, *Pray to Jesus for a miracle!* When I responded that I was already praying to Jesus, she replied, *Not your Jesus! Pray to my Lord and Savior Jesus Christ who died on the Cross!* The memory of her startling judgment of me and my Jesus led me to wonder if she had kept Katlyn from me by telling her negative things about my spiritual beliefs and my friends, particularly a dear friend of mine who followed Hindu and Buddhist teachings.

When I questioned her on this, she denied it. But my oldest son challenged her saying that she had told him negative things about my friend and me, so she surely must have told Katlyn as well. Then, just when I expected her to admit to this, she instead turned on me and said in an angry tone, *She practices witchcraft!* in reference to my friend. Once again in shock, I pleaded with her, *Do you even hear yourself? You have never even met her.* Exasperated by her response, I gave up trying to understand her. Imagine accusing someone else of practicing "witchcraft" after trying to bring Katlyn back from the dead while lying on top of her body and speaking in so-called "tongues." The hypocrisy is striking. I could now only guess the awful things she must have told Katlyn about me and my friend, as she clearly had lost her grasp on reality. I then decided that there was no more point in asking Katlyn's mother questions.

While I still couldn't understand the things that Katlyn's mother had said or done, I knew well that I would have treated Katlyn's situation completely differently. If I had learned of her rape three months earlier, I first would have held Katlyn in my arms, told her how much I loved her, and cried with her for all her pain and suffering, like I did when she called me in high school crying. I can't even imagine how violent and horrible it must have been for her, and how helpless and terrified for her life that she must have felt. After I helped her to feel loved and safe, I would have contacted a rape hotline for advice, and consulted with a doctor and therapist to discuss potential courses of action. Rape is a very violent, physical assault that often leads to severe depression and anxiety attacks, which are exactly the symptoms Katlyn was suffering from when she returned home from Hawaii. I can't imagine any scenario in which I would not have gotten Katlyn into some form of professional treatment for this and then monitored her closely until she was well again.

Regarding Katlyn's antidepressant medication, I certainly would not have allowed her to increase it without first contacting the doctor as it's illegal to change prescription medication without the doctor's orders. My advice to Katlyn was always to get the healing she needed so she could stop taking this dangerous medication. Under these circumstances, a doctor should have put Katlyn under 24-hour observation before making such an increase, as this is normal protocol for someone in severe depression. Katlyn's new medication dose of 40 mg was the maximum dose allowed for a full grown adult, while Katlyn was only 5 feet 2 inches tall and 110 pounds. Further, the warnings for this medication clearly describe the increased suicide risk, especially for young adults and when under increased stress. They also say to contact a healthcare provider immediately if a family member has thoughts about suicide.

After learning of Katlyn's suicidal thoughts, I would have immediately contacted a suicide hotline and taken Katlyn directly to a hospital. Knowing only too well her history of anxiety and depression, and fearing the increased suicide side effects of her antidepressant medication as mentioned earlier, I would not have taken any risks. The correct approach to suicidal thoughts can be found from multiple sources on the Internet such as the National Institute of Mental Health. They say in part, *If you know someone who may be considering suicide, do not leave him or her alone. Try to get your loved one to seek immediate help from a doctor or the nearest hospital emergency room, or call 911. Remove access to firearms or other potential tools for suicide, including medications.*

Regarding the "breaking off the shame" ritual, I would never have placed any blame, judgment or added shame on Katlyn regarding the rape or her sexual practices afterward. For me, it is immediately obvious how unloving, unfair, and damaging this would be to any rape victim, and even more so from a parent to a daughter. It is still incomprehensible to me that this was done in order to "help" Katlyn. How could they have been so out of touch with Katlyn's real needs? Rape guidelines are also widely available on the Internet and they state, in part, *Communicate without judgment.* Tell them, *It is not your fault.* The biggest issues for a rape survivor are trauma from the physical assault, guilt, and shame. The prayer ritual most likely made her shame and depression worse. It is common for rape survivors to suffer from Post Traumatic Stress Disorder (PTSD), and Katlyn had many of the symptoms - anxiety attacks, severe stomach pains, migraine headaches. PTSD is also known to greatly increase the risk of suicide.

Even with the new information provided by her mother, I struggled to understand how Katlyn could have come to the decision to end her life. In the search for better understanding, I retrieved all of her medical records, spoke with most of her closest friends, and researched books on sexual assault, trauma, and suicide. During this process, a good friend of Katlyn's told me that when she first told her mother about the rape in September, *Katlyn could tell her mother had disgust for her. She could feel it. She thought her mother would hug and kiss her and tell her it would be ok, but she did not. Katlyn went back to her room and cried because all she wanted was love.* My heart broke to hear this and feel the pain that Katlyn must have felt. But as heartbreaking as it was to think of the pain Katlyn felt at her mother's response, I could also see that it was consistent with the way her mom had described Katlyn's "immoral" sexual practices at the hospital in justifying her decision to "break off" Katlyn's shame.

Another of Katlyn's friends told me that Katlyn had gone quiet around Thanksgiving and after repeatedly asking her what was wrong, Katlyn finally replied on the Sunday after saying, *Something happened yesterday.* Katlyn explained that when she asked for her mother's help with her rape and depression, her mother said, *Things like this don't happen to good girls. Girls do not behave like that unless the devil is inside of them.* According to Katlyn's friend, her mother's "prayer circle" had performed the breaking off the shame ritual on Katlyn that Saturday after Thanksgiving. And although Katlyn's friend didn't know details of what happened, the idea that her mother blamed Katlyn for her rape and told her she was controlled by a devil seems completely consistent with her previously expressed views of Katlyn and her religious beliefs. But Katlyn was deeply wounded and vulnerable, and already filled with shame and feelings of worthlessness because of her rape. The last thing she needed was more judgment and shame.

If these statements are true, and I have no reason to believe they are not, I could see how this judgment by her mother and her church might have pushed Katlyn into a dark hole that she could never climb out of. Katlyn was apparently told that her "sickness" was caused by a "demon" that she herself had let in by being a "bad girl." This led to her "shame," which now had to be "broken off" of her. It would be difficult to imagine a more cruel and abusive thing to say to a rape victim. Even the name of this ritual sounds violent, like the sexual trauma she was suffering from. Katlyn's healing was dependent on getting this devil out of her, which in turn depended on the prayers of her mother and her church group, and ultimately on the will of God. And if she didn't get better, then Katlyn's only possible conclusion would be that she was unworthy, even in the eyes of God. At that point, I could see how she decided her life was hopeless.

There are other signs that point to this version of Katlyn's final days. One of Katlyn's college friends told me how disturbed she was when Katlyn's mother approached a group of them after the funeral service and said, *In her last days, Katlyn was with the Lord, trying to get her demons away by talking in tongues.* In addition, when I searched Katlyn's phone I found two text messages that reinforce this scenario. In one, Katlyn asks a woman from her mother's church group, who was very close to her mom and part of her "prayer circle," and whose teenage son had committed suicide years earlier, to come over and pray with her, this just three days before her suicide. There were no other texts like this, asking for prayers, in Katlyn's text history. Her mom's friend is working from home that evening and tells Katlyn she can't come pray with her.

The next day, two days before her suicide, Katlyn texts to her mother, *I want my old self back. I need a miracle.* Her mother responds, *Do u need anything from market basket* (the food store)*?* Katlyn replies, *I don't even want to eat.* Her mother's reply seems completely insensitive to what was an obvious cry for help. Katlyn's text that she needed "a miracle" shows that she was desperately looking for divine intervention and had no other hope. The text that she wanted her "old self back" likely refers to Katlyn's desire to be free of the devil. The day after these texts, her mom stays home from work due to Katlyn's suicidal thoughts. The day after that, her mother returns to work and Katlyn takes her life.

Once I put this all together and realized what had most likely driven Katlyn to take her life, I went into a dark hole myself. I felt the horrible pain and confusion of my beautiful little girl who had been violently raped, was deeply wounded, and only wanted to be loved, but instead had judgment and shame heaped upon her. She must have felt worthless and hopeless, and saw no way out once she was told there was a devil inside of her. My own pain at this realization felt unbearable and I became despondent. I could not speak. I lay there in bed, hopeless and helpless. I saw no way out. I believed that I felt what Katlyn must have felt, as I would have welcomed death at that moment. Thank God that my wife laid beside me and held me, and told me she would bring me to the hospital if my condition did not improve. Fortunately my desperate feelings passed by the next morning. I only wish that I had the chance be with Katlyn and hold her during her darkest moments because I would have never let her go and she would still be here with me.

Sexual Assault

I learned from a friend that Katlyn's sexual assault happened about two months after she moved to Hawaii, at a neighbor's house where she attended a party. There had been a lot of drinking and drug use. Katlyn went upstairs to "sleep off" her intoxication when her neighbor came in the room and assaulted her. Katlyn told a friend that she was so frightened that she couldn't move. In my attempts to better understand what Katlyn must have gone through, I found an extremely helpful book on sexual trauma called, *Life, Reinvented – A Guide to Healing from Sexual Trauma for Survivors and Loved Ones,* by Erin Carpenter, a licensed psychotherapist. She explains what it feels like to experience sexual trauma, *You feel as if something very wrong has just happened. Your boundaries are violated. You feel dirty, used, confused, and unsteady. You feel intense blame and shame. You feel alone and isolated. It feels like you can't tell anyone.* This explains why it took sixteen months for Katlyn to tell her mother, and then only at the strong urging of a girlfriend who had also experienced sexual trauma.

Another friend said Katlyn blamed herself for drinking too much alcohol, partying with the wrong people, and not fighting off the attacker or reporting the assault. Ms. Carpenter states that for most sexual assault victims, the guilt and self-blame over the assault morphs into deep shame, where we feel horrible not just about what we did, but about *who we are.* At the deepest level we feel like *we are the problem.* Carpenter states, *Shame is the feeling that we do not belong in the world, and that if others really saw us and our fundamental flaws, that we would be rejected.* This passage seems to describe what actually occurred with Katlyn. She had clearly decided that she did not belong in this world. And she had to feel fundamentally flawed and rejected, especially after she was told there was a demon in her that she had let in by being a bad girl.

One of the most serious problems for survivors of sexual assault, then, is the tendency of others to blame the victim. A common belief is that the victim is partly responsible, as they should never have put themself in the position to be raped, or at least should have put a stop to the assault. However, sexual assault is most often carried out by someone the victim knows, and trusting a person you know is hardly a character flaw. And the "freezing" type of involuntary response that Katlyn experienced is common during sexual assault, as our brain paralyzes our body to protect us. Still many cultures punish and ostracize rape victims and some even force them to marry the perpetrator. We think this terrible bias against the rape victim only exists in undeveloped countries, but the disgust shown by Katlyn's mother along with her judgment that Katlyn had become immoral after her rape and needed religious purification is the same type of bias, and could only have reinforced Katlyn's feeling of deep shame and unworthiness. Instead of more blame, the rape victim desperately needs love, compassion, and understanding.

As we discussed earlier in the book, when a loved one has deep emotional wounds, which is what sexual trauma causes, they first need to feel safe. Holding our loved one in our arms may be the most important first step in helping to restore their feeling of safety. This is what Katlyn told her friend she wanted when she first told her mother. Then the rape victim needs someone to *accept them as they are and just listen to them with empathy for their suffering.* As friends, family members or parents of a sexual assault victim, the worst thing we could do is try to "fix" them. This feels like rejection to the victim and reinforces the idea that they are "broken." We also don't have the training to understand what they have been through and what they need to heal. Even a qualified therapist would never treat a friend or family member as this would violate standards regarding the necessary boundaries between a therapist and client.

And while prayers may be helpful for those who have experienced sexual trauma, if we offer prayers as the *sole* remedy, we reinforce the victim's feeling of helplessness because the answer to our prayers is not in our control. Sexual trauma is by definition something terrible that happened which was out of our control, and research indicates that it is crucial that survivors take control of their own healing process so they learn *by experience* that they have the competency to go on. A qualified therapist would guide the trauma victim through a series of self-directed decisions and actions that would empower them to experience their own competency directly. Placing all hope for the survivor's healing on God's answer to our prayers takes away this vital element of self-control and disempowers the victim. It also raises more questions for the victim about their worthiness, such as, *Why would God even allow this to happen to me?* The most likely answer for the rape victim would be, *Because I am no good.*

Suicide

Research on suicide indicates that it is rarely caused by a single factor or event, but instead almost always occurs after a long history of psychological problems. This seems to be true with Katlyn. I recovered Katlyn's medical records from Hawaii and spoke to the doctor she saw immediately before she returned home. Katlyn's records from Hawaii indicate that just prior to returning home she was diagnosed with severe depression based on a standard screening questionnaire and was recommended for psychological counseling. In the questionnaire, Katlyn responded that she was feeling *down, depressed and hopeless - more than half the days,* and had *trouble sleeping and eating - nearly every day.* Katlyn also acknowledged that she had been treated for depression since 2009. When asked if she had *thoughts of hurting herself,* Katlyn responded, *Not at all,* and added, *I wouldn't do that to my family.*

When I spoke with her doctor from Hawaii, she was extremely sorry to hear about Katlyn, as she remembered Katlyn very well and had strong feelings for her. In the doctor's words, *There was something achingly beautiful and vulnerable and delicate about her.*

She reminded me of my own daughter and I wanted to keep her safe. The doctor added, *She seemed so lost, but seemed so sweet. She needed help.* The doctor said that Katlyn did not mention her prior sexual assault, but was aware that she needed help for her depression. The doctor said she waited around after Katlyn's appointment to speak directly with Katlyn's mother because she wanted to make sure Katlyn had someone to help get her home as soon as possible. When I asked the doctor if she thought Katlyn was suicidal at the time, but had lied on the questionnaire, the doctor said, *I feel something changed. She really did not intend to hurt herself. I don't believe she was lying to me.*

The doctor's final words to me were, *I am so sorry, she was beautiful, she was beautiful.* With my heart once again breaking and tears rolling down my face, I couldn't help but contrast the doctor's view of Katlyn with that of her mother. After less than an hour with Katlyn, the doctor saw her as, *achingly beautiful and vulnerable and delicate,* and was completely focused on protecting her and keeping her safe, like Katlyn was her own daughter. At the same time her mother saw Katlyn as a bad girl being controlled by a devil who had brought this suffering upon herself. I could now see why Katlyn was so upset at her mother for not offering any help after talking with this doctor. Katlyn said her mom had told her, *Just do what you want;* after which she called me for a plane ticket home. In a previous chapter we discussed how a person filled with love and light can immediately see this in another, and a person filled with judgment and hate can project that upon the most innocent of souls. These two starkly differing views of Katlyn and her suffering demonstrate this truth very clearly.

In order to prevent suicide, we need to better understand it. Two of Katlyn's closest friends were extremely surprised by her suicide based on how she had behaved around them. Her college boyfriend said, *Three different girls told me that Katlyn saved their lives by keeping them from suicide. That is not Katlyn.* And a close girlfriend who lifeguarded with Katlyn for several summers told me, *We once discussed the suicide of someone we knew and Katlyn said she would NEVER do that because it is the most selfish and hurtful thing you could do to your family.* But the decision to commit suicide is not straightforward. In a book called *The Psychology of Suicide,* by Edwin Schneidman, Ph.D., Norman Faberow, Ph.D., and Robert Litman, M.D., the authors make the case that *even the most ardent death wish is ambivalent.* People who contemplate suicide are undecided about living and dying, and most always look for a way out until the end. They have often made previous unsuccessful attempts at suicide, which is particularly true of women. Katlyn's apparent suicide attempt in college seemed ambivalent enough, as she did not take sufficient pills to cause any physical harm. But this was a serious warning just the same, and one that in hindsight we never responded to adequately.

According to Schneidman et al, eight out of ten people who kill themselves give warnings of their suicide intentions, as Katlyn had to her mother. Such warnings are an obvious cry for help and a search for an alternative. While suicide is most often premeditated, the act of suicide is usually an impulse decision. Schneidman's book states, *Most suicides occur within about three months following the beginning of "improvement," when the individual has the energy to put his morbid thoughts and feelings into effect.* It is chilling how this statement seems to parallel Katlyn's situation. She had come home from Hawaii two months earlier and initially seemed to be improving.

Over time, however, she became more depressed about being stuck at home and doubled her antidepressant medication at the suggestion of her mom. This likely gave her more strength, and perhaps enough to go through with her suicide. My assertion in college that I would rather *she never get out of bed,* instead of taking medication with a suicide side effect, seems prescient in hindsight. Katlyn still needed therapeutic help, more than ever, not more medication. In the end, the most important lessons of suicide prevention are simple and clear:

1) Take your friend or family member seriously.
2) Involve other people; don't try to handle the crisis alone.
3) Don't leave the person unless they are in the presence of trained professionals.

Another important lesson is that for women, sexual assault greatly increases the risk of suicide. Judith Herman, a former professor of Psychiatry at Harvard Medical School, notes in her groundbreaking book entitled, *Trauma and Recovery*, how strongly sexual trauma correlates to suicide attempts in women as follows: *Perhaps the most disturbing information on the long-term effects of traumatic events comes from a community study of crime victims, including 100 women who had been raped. The average time elapsed since the rape was nine years. Rape survivors reported more "nervous breakdowns," more suicidal thoughts, and more suicide attempts than any other group. While prior to the rape, they had been no more likely than anyone else to attempt suicide, almost one in five (19.2 percent) made a suicide attempt following the rape.*

Trauma

It is no surprise, then, that Katlyn was extremely vulnerable when she returned home from Hawaii, suffering not only from the serious trauma of her sexual assault, but also from the intense stress related to her prior work and living situations. Healing from trauma is difficult, however, as science has only recently recognized the extent to which trauma produces actual physiological changes in our brains that are not easily reversed. Dr. Bessel van der Kolk, a Harvard trained psychiatrist, is one of the world's leading researchers on trauma, founder and medical director of the Trauma Center in Brookline Massachusetts, and author of the book *The Body Keeps the Score - Brain, Mind, and Body in the Healing of Trauma*. In his book, Dr. van der Kolk states, *While we all want to move beyond trauma, the part of our brain that is devoted to ensuring our survival (deep below our rational brain) is not very good at denial. Long after the traumatic experience is over, it may be reactivated at the slightest hint of danger and mobilize disturbed brain circuits and secrete massive amounts of stress hormones. This precipitates unpleasant emotions, intense physical sensations, and impulsive and aggressive actions. These posttraumatic reactions feel incomprehensible and overwhelming. Feeling out of control, survivors of trauma often begin to fear they are damaged to the core and beyond redemption.*

Brain scans have shown that trauma changes our brain circuitry to make the right half, which processes emotions and feelings, dominant over the left half, which is logical and analytical. The connection pathway between the two brain halves is also degraded, so they can no longer communicate effectively to make sense of the world or what has happened. Therefore, the trauma victim loses much of their rational and verbal ability. In addition, the executive functioning part of their brain located in the prefrontal cortex, which allows us to sort through our thoughts, feelings, and emotions and make conscious choices, becomes largely shutdown. Thus, the trauma victim becomes mentally disabled, hyperreactive, and stuck either in fight or flight, or chronic shutdown. Dr. van der Kolk describes the reactive behavior resulting from these brain changes as follows, *These reactions are irrational and largely outside people's control. Intense and barely controllable urges and emotions make people feel crazy – and makes them feel like they don't belong to the human race... As a result, shame becomes the dominant emotion and hiding the truth the central preoccupation.*

Again, this seems to explain Katlyn's condition. Her brain seems to have been changed by trauma, causing her to suffer from uncontrollable emotional reactions and feel like she didn't belong on earth. *Shame had become the dominant emotion and hiding the truth the central preoccupation.* With this understanding, I could see why it took Katlyn so long to tell her mother about the rape and why she never told me. Her strong resistance to professional help also makes sense, as it's extremely difficult to discuss trauma because talking about it can cause one to re-experience the terrible pain and emotions, as though the trauma were actually happening again in that moment. And in many cases, trauma survivors literally don't have the words to describe their horrible experience. Therefore, the trauma survivor resists help out of self-defense, in fear that they would only be hurt even more. In Katlyn's experience telling her mother about her rape, this appears to be what occurred.

As acute as these trauma effects must have been for Katlyn after her rape, I had seen similar hyperreactive emotions in her for many years, along with an inability to verbalize her suffering and a strong resistance to professional therapy. Dr. van der Kolk's book also provides an explanation for this condition that takes us back to the wounded child discussion we started with at the beginning of this book. We know that as children, we are profoundly affected by the quality of the attachment relationship we have with our parents or caregivers, and that we carry these effects into adulthood. That is, if we have an insecure relationship with our parents, we will end up feeling insecure in our adult relationships. Research now shows that insecure attachment relationships in children can also lead to changes in the brain and resulting behavioral patterns that closely resemble the trauma related effects discussed above. This condition, caused by early childhood suffering and maltreatment, has been labeled Complex Trauma.

A landmark study on complex trauma, called the Adverse Childhood Experience (ACE) Study, was conducted by the Centers for Disease Control and Prevention (CDC) and Kaiser Permanente from 1995 through 1997. The ACE study asked over 17,000 patients to respond to questions about ten possible adverse childhood experiences, including physical and sexual abuse, emotional neglect, and family dysfunction, such as having parents who were divorced. The study scored each yes answer as one point and compared the total score (0 to 10) with the patient's detailed medical records to develop a correlation between their health and the number of adverse childhood experiences each patient encountered.

The results of this study were stunning. Most major public health problems were shown to increase directly with increasing ACE score, including chronic depression, alcoholism, obesity, smoking, suicide, domestic abuse, heart disease, and cancer. Dr. van der Kolk states that the leading researcher at the CDC, *realized that they had stumbled upon the gravest and most costly public health issue in the United States: child abuse. He had calculated that its overall costs exceeded those of cancer or heart disease and that eradicating child abuse in America would reduce the overall rate of depression by more than half, alcoholism by two-thirds, and suicide, IV drug use, and domestic violence by three-quarters. It would also have a dramatic effect on workplace performance and vastly decrease the need for incarceration.*

Katlyn had clearly suffered greatly as a child, beginning with the separation and divorce of her parents. In high school, she told me I had *ruined her life* when I left home and didn't return. No doubt this was the first major trauma in her life. Katlyn also experienced many smaller traumas growing up associated with her relationships, school, and work, as discussed earlier in this chapter. Lastly, Katlyn was subjected to long-term emotional abuse in the form of yelling at home. In our high school discussion, she said, *Mom yells at me because that is all she knows how to do when she gets mad.* Katlyn's college boyfriend recently told me that she continued to experience problems with her mother's anger in college, and had told him, *I hate being at home because I am always being screamed at.* This type of emotional abuse from a parent is exceptionally damaging for a developing child or young adult. Dr. van der Kolk states in his book on trauma, *Over the years our research team has repeatedly found that chronic emotional abuse and neglect can be just as devastating as physical abuse and sexual molestation.*

Dr. van der Kolk's description of childhood trauma and its profound effects made so much sense to me. I could finally understand why life had been so hard for Katlyn, and why getting her the help and healing she needed seemed so difficult. I could see, in hindsight, that her brain had likely changed over the years, as evidenced by her tendency to emotionally react or shutdown at the slightest injustice. Katlyn seemed to be stuck in self-defense mode because she lived in constant fear of being attacked. But this was not her fault and there was nothing she could do to control it.

I could also see that these likely changes to her brain from her childhood wounds kept her from seeking help, because there was no one she trusted or felt safe with. Katlyn's limited experience with therapy showed her that reliving her childhood trauma was just too painful. And all this was before she was raped. Acknowledging these truths now feels so sad and tragic to me, and once again makes my tears flow, because Katlyn was the most beautiful and innocent of souls, and I tried so hard to love her, understand her, and help her. But I really didn't know what was going on. And now it's too late. This is why our search for understanding is so critically important.

For those who recognize Katlyn's childhood trauma or behavior patterns in themselves or others, there is great hope. Medical science has developed a number a therapeutic approaches that are effective in treating event-based trauma, such as from rape or war, or the complex trauma that comes from an insecure or abusive childhood. While conventional talk therapy can be helpful, in many cases it is too difficult or not effective by itself. However, several other types of therapy have been shown to "rewire" the trauma-damaged brain and restore normal cognitive functionality. Many of them do not require the victim to discuss details from the trauma, sparing them from the pain of reliving it. While the details of these trauma therapies go beyond this scope of this book, I list some here that are discussed more fully in Dr. van der Kolk's book:

1) EMDR – eye movement desensitization and reprocessing
2) Trauma Sensitive Yoga
3) Internal Family Systems Therapy
4) Psychomotor Therapy
5) Neurofeedback Therapy
6) Therapeutic Theater Programs

Some of these trauma therapies, most notably EMDR, Trauma Sensitive Yoga, and Neurofeedback, seem to act directly to rewire and re-enable parts of the brain that were disabled by trauma, without much cognitive effort. However, research shows that all trauma survivors eventually need to take action to develop competencies and experience successes in order to come out of their fear and hopelessness, and restore their sense of power and agency. Dr. van der Kolk states, *Competence is the best defense against the helplessness of trauma.* With success at the regular tasks of living, such as jobs and relationships, they take back control. Katlyn seemed to instinctively know this, as she was constantly striving hard for success in her work and relationships, and after one-month home from Hawaii, when she felt herself drifting back into depression, she became desperate to return to Hawaii, though I didn't understand why at the time.

Trauma research has also shown that long-term healing requires the trauma victim to access their emotional wounds and find compassion for their own suffering, as we discussed earlier in this book. They need to learn that it was not their fault, let go of blame and self-hate, and eventually learn to love themselves. And with this realization from the science of trauma and healing, we seem to have come full circle. The emotional healing that Katlyn needed most is exactly what she had said, *I need to love myself a lot more. That's the biggest thing I need and then everything else will fall into place.* This work is exceptionally difficult, however, when our brain circuits are partially disabled by trauma. So for many victims of trauma, professional trauma therapy may be the only way to restore sufficient brain function to enable the emotional healing that is so desperately needed.

Answers to my Questions

My search for understanding helped me to answer some of the most difficult questions that I struggled with after Katlyn decided to leave this world. Those questions that were most important for me to answer follow.

Why didn't Katlyn also come to me for help with her rape or thoughts of suicide?

Sexual assault survivors have intense feelings of shame and greatly fear reliving the pain of their traumatic experience. It is therefore extremely difficult to discuss their rape with anyone. In growing up, Katlyn had seen doctors with her mother and learned to confide in her, so it was natural for Katlyn to speak to her mother first. In general, it would also be more difficult for a daughter to reveal that she had been sexually violated to her father. I always viewed Katlyn as pure and innocent, and had told her this since she was a little girl. Even in her struggles, Katlyn remained perfect in my eyes, and she knew this. As dirty, defiled, and shamed as she must have felt after the rape, I believe she feared that telling me would destroy my image of her and she would no longer be my innocent little girl.

Of course, this thought was not correct, as my view of Katlyn could never change, but Katlyn likely felt this way. In her book on sexual trauma, Ms. Carpenter tells us the rape victim believes, *if others really saw us and our fundamental flaws, we would be rejected.* I believe that deep down Katlyn felt like she had already lost me once as a child when I divorced her mother, and she was not willing to risk losing me again. The blame and shame that her mother put on Katlyn could only have made this feeling worse, and therefore harder for Katlyn to come to me. It is likely that in Katlyn's own mind, after her mother's prayer ritual, she had become the "devil girl." After reading Katlyn's text messages, I believe she was wounded and vulnerable enough to actually believe this. How do you face your loving father who holds you on a pedestal when you believe you have a demon inside you?

Additionally, I believe Katlyn feared a number of potential reactions from me, such as me confronting the perpetrator, trying to get her to inform police and press charges, or withdrawing my financial support for her in Hawaii and forcing her to return home. She would have viewed all of these actions as harmful to her, and potentially harmful to me as well, especially if I confronted the perpetrator. In choosing not to tell me, I believe she was trying to protect us both from pain and harm. Near the end, just before her suicide, when we spoke and agreed to get together to develop a plan for her to get back to Hawaii, I felt like she was being sincere. But by the next day when Katlyn said she wasn't feeling well and pushed our meeting off, in hindsight, she seemed to have given up. I believe she was too ashamed to tell me her thoughts of suicide and didn't feel strong enough to accept the help I offered. My only conclusion is that she could no longer see any possibility of recovery. If her mother was not willing to get her professional help for her suicide thoughts or inform me, she must have felt her situation was truly hopeless.

Why did Katlyn keep going back to her mother for help, even after being repeatedly hurt by her?

Children have a biological imperative to attach to their parents and will keep trying to get the love they need from them, regardless of how they are treated. We have no choice in this, as our instincts tell us we need the love of our parents to survive. This is why, as Dr. van der Kolk states, *Patients with abusive families keep going back to be hurt again.* Children also blame themselves for any dysfunction with their parents because the child cannot see their parents as defective, with their instincts again rejecting such a notion because the child's life depends upon their parents. Katlyn's behavior, then, appears consistent with what is known about child abuse and complex trauma. This explains why Katlyn felt unworthy and unlovable from her childhood experiences at home, because she was not able to put the blame on her mother or father.

In hindsight, the child's imperative to love and support even an abusive parent is clear to me in how Katlyn behaved. Katlyn would tell me how generous her mother was to others and was quick to make excuses for her, such as saying, *yelling is all she knows how to do,* even though her mother's yelling was terribly painful and damaging to her. Katlyn also pretended to adopt her mother's religious views only to please her and gain her love, as Katlyn never practiced them when away from home. In our discussions, it was clear that she was quite skeptical about religion. Yet Katlyn went through with their "breaking off the shame" ritual, asked for their prayers, wanted a "miracle" to help her heal, and if her mother can be believed, even "spoke in tongues." But this was most likely Katlyn pretending to believe in the hope she could finally get her mother's love and approval, because this is what a child needs to survive.

Why did Katlyn's mother neglect to get Katlyn professional help or tell me about her rape or thoughts of suicide?

This was the most difficult question for me to answer. After struggling for some months with it, I sent a long list of written questions to Katlyn's mother, telling her what I had heard from Katlyn's friends and others, asking her if what they said was true, and if so, why she would have behaved in this way. She did not respond, so I am left with only my direct experience with Katlyn's mother, information provided by others, and my reasoning in trying to answer this question.

One likely reason her mother did not get help for Katlyn is shame. Her mother was clearly ashamed of Katlyn and what had happened to her. The "breaking off the shame" ritual she performed on Katlyn is an obvious sign, particularly when she described the reason for the ritual as Katlyn having become sexually immoral after the rape. When I asked her mother if Katlyn had ever told her she was ashamed, she responded, *No.* This tells me two important things; first, the idea of shame came from her mother; and second, her mother never really listened to Katlyn, because if she had, Katlyn likely would have confessed that she blamed herself for the rape and felt terrible shame, as she had told a girlfriend. But in their first discussion about the rape, Katlyn felt nothing but *disgust* from her mother, as her friend told me, so Katlyn was not likely to confess her shame to her mother when she did not feel loved and safe.

When a parent is ashamed of their child, it means they have judged their child as deficient or defective, and what they care about most is how badly their child might reflect on them as the parent. Feeling ashamed is about the parent feeling this threat to their own self-esteem, and does not reflect any love or concern for their child. Katlyn's mother was always extremely concerned about what others thought about her and went to great efforts to project the perfect image. The idea that she couldn't bear to let others know Katlyn had been raped, outside of her small prayer circle, because this would reflect badly on her as Katlyn's mother makes sense to me.

Another reason to keep Katlyn from professional help and from me is that her mother needed Katlyn to need her. Their co-dependent relationship had been strained by Katlyn's years away in college and in Hawaii. Katlyn's rape and resulting severe depression provided an opportunity for her mother to manipulate Katlyn and make her dependent again. And with her mother being so needy, there was no room for Katlyn's needs to be met. This seemed to be the story of Katlyn's life.

There is no doubt that her mother knew Katlyn's condition was very serious. First, she had spoken with the doctor in Hawaii and was told that Katlyn was severely depressed and having anxiety attacks. Next, she could see Katlyn's suffering first hand, which is why she told Katlyn to double her antidepressant medication. Finally, she had invited one of her college friends who is a practicing family therapist to visit with her and Katlyn to discuss the rape. When I spoke with this friend after Katlyn's suicide, she candidly offered that she had experienced rape herself and had told Katlyn's mom that this was very serious and that Katlyn needed professional help right away. Her friend also told Katlyn's mother she was not qualified to provide Katlyn with this help. When her mother responded that she was waiting to get Katlyn insurance before seeing a doctor, the friend told me she urged her mother not to wait because she could see how badly Katlyn was suffering. Hearing these comments directly from her mother's close friend, and knowing that she contacted a trusted friend for help rather than another medical professional, tells me her mother was well aware of the seriousness of Katlyn's situation and was most likely trying to keep this situation quiet to protect her own image.

I believe another reason why Katlyn's mother did not get her help was that she blamed Katlyn for her problems and wanted to punish her. She had told Katlyn she was not a "good girl" anymore and told me Katlyn had become sexually immoral after the rape. Her mother also refused Katlyn's urgent request for help when she had her nervous breakdown in Hawaii just before returning home. Punishing Katlyn was a recurring theme for her mother and one she had discussed with me many times before, telling me how badly Katlyn behaved, and how I needed to stop being so supportive of Katlyn and come down harder on her. Punishment is also a cornerstone of her religious beliefs, with sinners always deserving their punishment, which in the worst case is burning in hell for eternity. Katlyn's mother had spent great effort lobbying members of my family against me to punish me after our separation. And she was always jealous of the close, loving relationship between Katlyn and me, as noted to me by several people who had observed this. So refusing to get Katlyn help or tell me about her problems served to punish us both.

I have also pondered long and hard about her mother's idea that Katlyn had a devil or demon in her. What I conclude is that, for Katlyn's mother and her church, "evil" is just another word for "hate." You need to have this "evil and hate" within you to project it upon another, especially one as pure and innocent as Katlyn. No one with love in their heart could look at Katlyn and see evil. Despite her deep wounds, she was as kind and loving as a person could be. The reaction of the doctor in Hawaii to Katlyn and the tributes to her in this book show this truth. After her rape, Katlyn was desperately in need of love, compassion and understanding. There was nothing evil about her. She had not become immoral. She was completely blameless. All she wanted and needed was to be loved and accepted, but her mother had another agenda.

Her mother's church preaches love for all those that adhere to their teachings, but then labels the things they think are wrong as evil, such as my friend whom Katlyn's mother had labeled as a witch without having met her. The church gave her mother the love and acceptance she craved, while at the same time, providing her with a free license to hate. Church followers are encouraged to see a devil at work in everything they despise, which is why Katlyn's mother believed she saw the devil in her.

Her mother had a love-hate relationship with Katlyn, but was apparently unable to admit this hate to herself. She yelled and screamed at Katlyn because there were parts of her that she hated.

So she labeled this part of Katlyn as "evil," invented a devil, and then it became acceptable to hate part of her own daughter, because it was not Katlyn she hated, but the devil within her. Blaming this situation on the devil had the added benefit of absolving her from any responsibility as Katlyn's mother. This would explain why the only people she could tell were church friends who would also see Katlyn's situation as the work of the devil. The problem with that logic, however, is there was never any devil in Katlyn, but only the hate that her mother had projected upon her. And Katlyn could feel her mother's hate, even if her mother had fooled herself by calling it a devil.

This becomes apparent when we remember how Katlyn had felt her mother's "disgust" after she told her about the rape, and how Katlyn's mother had described her sexual relationships after her rape as immoral. Her mother said this was why she decided to "break off" Katlyn's shame. I want to repeat a tribute shared earlier from Katlyn's Hawaii boyfriend, which discusses his experience in one of these so-called "immoral" sexual relationships cited by her mother:

You have forever changed my life. You were my light in the darkness shining bright. The world is truly not the same without you. You were my best friend, inspiration, confidant, and partner. You paddled into my life one day and have forever changed who I am. Through your love, prayers, and unwavering support you helped me through some of my life's hardest battles. I thank God for every second I was blessed to spend with you.

Can you imagine Katlyn hearing that the sex she had in this relationship was immoral, especially when she was suffering from severe depression while trying to recover from the deep trauma and shame of her rape? The previously mentioned book from Erin Carpenter on sexual assault states that the first sexual relationship after a rape can be extremely healing. I witnessed their relationship during two separate week-long visits in Hawaii, something Katlyn's mother had never done, and there was clearly a very sweet and loving bond between them. But her mother put shame on this relationship by imposing a moral standard on Katlyn regarding sex that she herself had not lived up to either prior to or during our marriage. This was not only reckless, given Katlyn's medical condition, but also extremely hypocritical.

In the humility chapter, we discussed how research shows that in order to commit an atrocity, you need to have extreme overconfidence and believe you have a moral mandate. For me, what happened to Katlyn was an atrocity. It started with her rape, but there was so much that could have been done afterward to help Katlyn. Instead, her mother chose the moral mandate of her church to blame Katlyn's suffering on her own bad behavior and the evil demon residing within her. Then her mother had the extreme overconfidence to believe it was her role to fix Katlyn by driving this demon out of her. In her self-righteousness and arrogance, she took on the role of mother, father, therapist, doctor, and even God, despite Katlyn's obvious and desperate need for outside help.

During a family discussion days after Katlyn's death, the church pastor who would later perform Katlyn's funeral service admonished her mother for stating that, *God had failed her,* in reference to Katlyn's suicide. The pastor said this was like a man who prayed for something to eat but then refused to get up and go to work. In other words, we are responsible for the consequences of our actions or inactions, not God. But Katlyn's mother was unable to accept any responsibility for Katlyn's suicide, so she blamed God, because He was supposed to remove the devil from Katlyn after she had correctly prayed for this. For her mother, it was no doubt the same devil that caused Katlyn to kill herself, not the severe depression and anxiety Katlyn felt after being raped, or anything her mother had done or not done in response.

Just when I thought things could not possibly get worse, weeks after Katlyn's suicide I got more disturbing news. My two siblings who had helped Katlyn's mother convert to her extreme righteous religious beliefs over fifteen years earlier told another family member that they wanted to get together and pray because my friend, the one who Katlyn's mother said practiced witchcraft, was making *inroads into the family.* My two siblings apparently had determined, along with Katlyn's mother, that the demon in Katlyn that caused her to commit suicide had come from my friend, whom neither of them had met. Of course, they also never spoke to me about this. It's hard for me to imagine how after losing my daughter, in their blind self-righteousness, my own siblings could act to harm me further, all while pretending to be loving and supportive to my face. This was not the humility my parents had taught us and demonstrated by their example. As Katlyn would say about things that were terribly wrong, *That's so messed up.*

The behavior of Katlyn's mother and my siblings shows why humility is so important. If they had kept their false beliefs to themselves, and Katlyn's mother had done the minimal things that common sense and humility would dictate, such as contact medical professionals and inform me, Katlyn would still be alive. The danger, then, was not that her mother had false beliefs, but that she was so overconfident in her beliefs that she projected them on Katlyn and used them to manipulate Katlyn for her own purposes, while at the same time ignoring Katlyn's well-being. This is what Muslim extremists do with disaffected youths to turn them into suicide bombers. And the results are identical, as it's always the helpless innocents that are lost while the real evil remains.

Those who are filled with love could not shine anything but love and light on another, even those that are deeply wounded and confused. Authentic love never comes in the form of self-righteousness. As Mother Teresa said, *It is in being humble that our love becomes real.* When love recognizes evil, it offers only compassion, because only light can overcome darkness. Love does not fear evil and does not speak of evil because that only empowers it. In order to call another person evil, the evil must reside within you first. Then you can project this onto the most pure and innocent of souls, as was done to Katlyn. In this case, "evil" was just another word for hate and intolerance. And those who are pointing out evil all around them are the ones who are actually spreading it.

Lessons

Katlyn had deep emotional wounds from her childhood that were never addressed. It started when I left home to try and create a better life for us and continued as her mother told her bad things about me and emotionally abused her with her judgments and yelling. Katlyn's difficult experiences at school, work, and among friends just reinforced her insecurities. Katlyn seemed to have nowhere she felt safe. We now know how harmful such trauma can be to a child. The resulting emotional damage is no different than that caused by physical or sexual abuse.

Katlyn's repeated traumas seemed to have physiologically changed her brain structure, making her hyperreactive and prone to emotional responses, while at the same time diminishing her capability for rational thought. When this happens, we feel hopeless to understand or control ourselves and resist therapeutic help out of fear of being hurt even more. Even though she felt deeply wounded, a part of Katlyn still seemed to believe she was a good person and was strong enough to attain her goals. Katlyn seemed determined to prove to herself and to us that she could make it on her own. After she moved to Hawaii, she encountered perhaps the worst trauma possible for her, a sexual assault. She initially confided only to her closest friend, but after nearly 16 months of suffering from PTSD like symptoms, Katlyn finally gained the courage to ask for help.

When Katlyn asked her mother for help, she encountered more judgment, shame, and trauma. Although she had come home from Hawaii for family support and healing, she became even more depressed. Shortly after a sharp increase in her antidepressant medication and a religious ritual conducted by her mother to remove her shame, Katlyn concluded her life was hopeless, even though she had family and friends who loved her dearly and other options available for help that she did not explore. In her final days, Katlyn resisted my repeated attempts to see her, most likely because of her intense feelings of shame and a belief that she was worthless and could not be helped.

Many of the points in previous chapters seem to be illustrated by this story. Katlyn had a clear and unmet need for love and connection, acceptance and understanding, and emotional healing. She had grown up with an insecure attachment relationship with both of her parents through no fault of her own. Like most victims of child abuse, Katlyn had extremely low self-esteem. As a result, Katlyn resisted professional help because her wounds were too painful and she never felt safe. At times it seemed like she was making progress by attaining some success in the world, but then another traumatic event would occur and she would once again feel like things could never go right for her. Her sexual assault, which is one of the most despicable, violent, acts of self-gratification that one person could perpetrate on another, seemed to be the one trauma that Katlyn ultimately could not overcome without professional help.

An important lesson of this tragedy, then, is that we all should have sought help sooner. I should have entered joint therapy with Katlyn long ago, after our separation, when I could see she was struggling to understand and accept that I still loved her. Katlyn, for her part, should not have resisted my many attempts to get her help, and when she finally did ask for help with the trauma from her sexual assault, she should have sought help from me and from medical professionals. As painful as this prospect may have seemed to Katlyn at the time, the alternative path she chose ended up much worse.

Regarding her mother, instead of getting professional help for her insecurities and depression long ago, she seemed to regress over the years by adopting extremely righteous religious views that blocked out her insecurities and provided her with more reasons to blame me for her suffering and keep Katlyn from me. Her mother's belief system also taught her to define Katlyn's sexual trauma and severe depression in moralistic terms of judgment, shame, and evil demonic influences and to address this life-threatening problem solely by invoking the power of God to cast the demons out.

Such terrible confusion, where Katlyn's mother blocked out all common sense and concern for Katlyn in favor of her own twisted religious agenda, is difficult to accept. It feels like it must be a bad dream because it couldn't possibly be true. But when I keep waking up and Katlyn is still gone, and the actions leading up to her suicide were confessed by her mother, I realize how negligent and reckless a parent can be with their child. Even though we see examples of this in the news, you never believe it could happen to your child. As it turns out, Katlyn's suicide is not what was unimaginable after all, but rather the events leading up to it.

In the end, I feel equally responsible for Katlyn's loss because I was far too naïve as her father. All these years I tried to never say a bad word about Katlyn's mother or tell my children the truth about her because I thought this could only harm them. But on this point, while my intentions were good, my approach was wrong. I never anticipated that Katlyn's mother could continue to hold such negativity about me for so long and put this on my children, or could treat Katlyn with the same type of emotional abuse that she had placed on me. I should have known better and worked to show my children the truth about her, even though it may have been very painful for them at the time.

In a real sense, I had abandoned them to figure out their mother on their own. It was my responsibility to protect Katlyn, even if it was from her mother, and in that responsibility, I failed. By the time Katlyn told me what was going on with her mother in high school, the emotional damage had already been done. When Katlyn refused my attempts to get her professional help in college, I then chose to let her go on with her life and believe that over time my loving support would be enough to help her heal. But this was again naïve, as life kept dealing her more traumatic experiences and my love by itself would not be enough to heal her deep emotional wounds. Although now I know better, as I have said earlier, it is too late for Katlyn.

Humility, humility, humility…if only we all had it sooner. It takes humility to ask for help, either that or extreme suffering and pain, which our therapeutic medications mask. Asking for help is not a sign of weakness, but a sign of strength. And we are so much stronger and resilient that we realize. It's the fear of looking at our pain that paralyzes us, but the truth we try to avoid is liberating. Once we see the truth, we are no longer floundering in ignorance and confusion. Armed with the truth, we can make a conscious, empowered choice to change ourselves and our lives. While it may require great courage to ask for help and face the truth, or speak the truth even when you know it will be painful (as it has been in writing this book), there is no other way to healing. As Jesus says in the Gospel of John, *The truth will set you free.*

I wish I had asked for help and reached these understandings about myself, Katlyn, and her mother sooner, because if I had, Katlyn would likely still be with us. I offer our story in the hope that it leads others to get the help they need sooner in order to reduce their suffering, get the healing they need, and prevent such a tragedy. In this way, we could love and honor the life of my precious little Katlyn together.

Katlyn had this amazing light within her since she was a child, and it was always there, visible to those who had the same light within them. But she encountered so much darkness in life, as many of us do, and in the end, this darkness eventually snuffed out Katlyn's beautiful light. There are many people and institutions in our world that preach about love, but instead practice hate and intolerance, and in this way their darkness masquerades as light. So, in our search for love and acceptance, we need the courage to look at our own dark side and need to be very careful of who and what we follow, because darkness and light cannot coexist. This quote from Dr. Martin Luther King, Jr. speaks to this truth:

Darkness cannot drive out darkness; only light can do that.
Hate cannot drive out hate; only love can do that.

Conclusion

Imagine all the people, living life in peace. You may say I'm a dreamer, but I'm not the only one. I hope some day you'll join us, then the world will be as one.

—John Lennon

This picture is the last one I have of Katlyn and me together, along with my oldest son and Katlyn's dog, Teddy. It was taken in late October 2014 after a road race. I had been training hard for three years to run a 5K race in under twenty minutes, which I had not done for two decades. Katlyn and her brother came to cheer me on. They were on the course screaming for me in the final third of the race when I needed it most. When I succeeded in reaching my goal with a few seconds to spare, they were both so happy and proud of me. You can just see it in their faces. This is the way it always was when Katlyn, her brothers, and I got together. Our times were filled with joy and laughter. My two sons are my best friends and Katlyn was the love of my life. There was no place I felt happier or more content than with them. Having developed this wonderful relationship with my sons and Katlyn, it felt impossible to accept her choice to leave us just six weeks later. I had no idea how to go on without her.

I spent each day grieving her loss and praying for any sign that Katlyn was okay. This may not make sense to a person without faith in an afterlife, but I felt desperate to connect with Katlyn somehow and know that she had arrived safely in the arms of God. I had great trouble eating, sleeping, and just getting through each day. I felt extremely vulnerable and had frequent bouts with uncontrollable tears and anxiety. I went to the ocean each day, as this is where Katlyn was the happiest, and spent time walking and talking to her there. In my attempt to figure out how to go on without Katlyn, I leaned heavily on my wife, who also needed me to get through this. Together, my wife and sons gave me reasons to keep living. But there was little else left in my life that mattered.

Nine days after her death, Katlyn came to me in a vivid dream at around three o'clock in the morning. I had chills throughout my body, was feeling "pins and needles" from head to toe, and saw her clearly as she spoke to me. Katlyn first hugged me deeply while putting her head on my chest, and then told me not to worry because she was no longer suffering. Her loving embrace along with the words that she was okay, were the best gifts she could have given me. Katlyn then said she could see the truth now, *all the truths I wanted to tell her about how to get the help she needed.* Katlyn said she understood what her mother had done to her and then left me with these words, *Anger and negative emotions are toxic, poison to those who hold them and those they are visited upon.*

I immediately wrote down the details of this dream in my journal, and it gave me some relief to have heard from Katlyn in a way that seemed very real to me. But the day-to-day reality of life without Katlyn was still brutally difficult for me. As I dealt with feelings of extreme grief, guilt, and heartbreak, I realized that I needed to do something to honor Katlyn and tell her story, like grieving parents often do when they lose a child. On Christmas Day 2014, I decided to finish this book in honor of Katlyn and wrote in my journal, *This I will do For the Love of Katlyn - Devote my life to healing the world.* This is what Katlyn wanted most for herself and others, and so in honoring her, I could do no less.

Actually writing this book so soon after Katlyn's suicide was quite difficult, however, as I struggled with all the horrible feelings churning inside. To help manage my stress, I kept up my morning and evening practice, and relied heavily on my journaling. There was so much pain and emotion inside me that it didn't seem fair to put that on my loved ones. So my journal became my outlet. In late January 2015, during my morning meditation, almost two months after Katlyn passed, I was still wondering how I could possibly finish the book when I heard Katlyn's voice in my mind say, *Don't worry about the book Daddy, just show up, surrender, and serve.* And so this became my writing practice. Just showing up each morning, trying to let go of (i.e. surrender) my negative feelings and emotions, asking for God's help in writing a book that would best serve others, and then seeing what was there to write. This is when the book unexpectedly began to flow.

In mid-February 2015, Katlyn came to me in another vivid dream around 3:00am and said, *Daddy, wake up and write this down! We're together, we're together, we're together. Don't forget! We're together always!* I did what I was told and wrote Katlyn's words in my bedside journal right away. With this dream, it seemed as though Katlyn was trying to tell me she was with me all the time now. And though I still felt mostly pain from her loss, there seemed to be a growing connection to her as well. Katlyn had seemingly spoken to me three times in the past three months. Each time the voice in my mind sounded like Katlyn's voice. The words felt like her words. It felt so real and also made some sense to me, as my goal in helping others and bringing healing to the world was the same as hers. Now I started each day of my writing with the annotation:

S3-KWM-☺, which was my way of reminding myself to, *Show up, surrender, and serve; Katlyn is with me; Smile.*

There is a well-known phenomenon in writing or other art forms like music and dance, where our conscious mind becomes quiet and an external creative force seems to take over. It's often called "being in the zone" or "writing in flow." This was my experience in writing most of this book. I was completely absorbed in the process and the words came forth effortlessly, sometimes as though I was taking dictation. The writing felt like a special gift to me, one to be shared with others. I soon realized that to make the book most helpful for others, I would need to share part of my life story and part of Katlyn's as well. I was reluctant to do this, as I felt vulnerable and could see the many mistakes I had made. But with my heart broken wide open, I could also see that we all suffer from the same wounds and make the same mistakes trying to get the love we need. So in honor of Katlyn and with her as my inspiration, I decided to humbly offer our life experiences, no matter how messy, in hopes that the reader would see their own struggles in our struggles and learn by our example so as to avoid making the same mistakes.

Although most of the book seemed to flow to me, I still had many moments of doubt. When the book was about two-thirds complete, I shared the partial manuscript with a friend who was having relationship struggles and called to ask me for help. Just hours later, while I was wondering if I had done the right thing, I heard Katlyn's voice again, as though she was right next to me, saying in a sad tone, *What if I had that?* I stopped in my tracks, had chills go through my entire body, and began to cry, feeling so moved to hear Katlyn's voice in my mind, seemingly filled with regret for the misunderstandings that caused her to leave. I was grateful to receive her message that the understanding in this book is what she needed, and if she had it sooner, she would still be alive. It felt like Katlyn had come to give me the courage I needed to continue and finish what I had started in her honor.

Within three months, I had finished writing the *LAUGH* and Practice chapters of the book and all that remained was telling Katlyn's story. This is the point where I obtained her medical records and began talking to her friends to see if I could come to some greater understanding of why Katlyn left us. As more information came in, I grew more and more depressed, because the facts were more horrible than I had imagined. Again, I had serious doubts if I could write about this.

Then in late April 2015, Katlyn again came to me in a powerful, vivid, dream, and said, *I have been shamed, framed, and blamed for a crime that I didn't commit and it is up to you to push back and defend me.* Katlyn then said, *Write what my girlfriends told you, because it is all true.* Lastly, she said, *You are the only one left to make my victim statement. The truth needs to come out. This is 'Katlyn's Justice!'*

Once again I had received a jolt of courage and purpose that seemingly had come directly from Katlyn. I wrote the details of the dream down immediately. And although I was more committed than ever to finishing the book, my writing ground to a halt in May 2015 while I tried to deal with my own intense feelings. I sought medical attention and was diagnosed with PTSD, still suffering greatly from the trauma of losing Katlyn, now combined with the trauma of learning details of the horrible circumstances that preceded her suicide. I was filled with grief and anger at Katlyn's mother, and many times thought I felt Katlyn's rage. My physical symptoms—anxiety attacks, emotional breakdowns, stomach pains, and nightmares—got worse. This is when I became despondent, as mentioned earlier, and lost my will to live. Without the steady love and support from my wife, I'm not sure I would have made it. Even with her support, recovery from this place took a great deal of help and effort.

I knew my anger and negative emotions could kill me if I didn't find a way to let them go. So I meditated, prayed, and journaled each day, saw a therapist and psychiatrist, and leaned on a wider circle of family and friends, all in the hope of finding some healing and relief. But in the end, it was not those efforts, but instead my Katlyn who saved me. Months later, in September 2015, she came to me during my morning meditation and told me (by her voice in my mind) that she had forgiven her mother because her mom was deeply wounded and confused. Katlyn said I needed to see her mother in this same way and find compassion for her mom's suffering, just as I had found compassion for her (Katlyn).

As I was still filled with anger and blame toward her mother, this did not seem possible to me, so I asked Katlyn how to do this. She said I had, *all the love I needed within me and it was just a choice to find compassion for her mother, a choice I needed to keep making each day.* Katlyn reminded me of Jesus' words while dying on the cross, *Forgive them Father for they know not what they do.* This was the example Katlyn wanted me to follow. She told me to ask God for help and it would be there. And with that, Katlyn's simple words of wisdom broke me out of my victim mentality and empowered me to make a more loving choice. For the love of my Katlyn, this is the choice I have been trying to make each day since.

With Katlyn's wisdom and my more loving choice, it became possible to finish this book, while also trying to stay true to the same *LAUGH* principles that I was teaching. The intense feelings of anger and blame remained inside me, but they weakened as I finally put Katlyn's story on paper. This, unexpectedly, became the path to releasing much of my suffering. In writing the truth of Katlyn's life and death, and offering it as a gift to others, our suffering now had a higher purpose. I could see how Katlyn's story might help save other young people who suffered like her, or help parents like me to avoid making similar mistakes. And with these thoughts I found some relief, believing that Katlyn's life and suffering would not have been wasted.

The importance of making the right choice also became apparent. When we suffer from great injustice, we can choose to remain in a victim mode and find endless reasons to blame and hate others. This is what many people and organizations help us do and exactly what Katlyn's mother had done in keeping Katlyn from getting the help she needed after her rape. As Katlyn said in my first dream, *Anger and negative emotions are toxic, poison to those who hold them and those they are visited upon.* But no matter how grave the injustice, we can always try to make the loving choice of seeing the perpetrator with compassion in recognizing they are wounded and confused, like the wounded child we discussed at the beginning of the book. It is always hurt people that hurt others.

We may need to defend ourselves or withdraw from a relationship that is harmful to us, but we should also try to release our anger and blame, and make the compassionate choice to not wish the responsible person harm. I have found greater acceptance and peace now in learning this lesson from Katlyn and in choosing to practice it each day. At first I thought it would be impossible, but over time realized I had this power within me. We all do, whether we think of this power as our higher self, inner Buddha, or the love of God. Along with our wounds, we always have the power to make a loving choice within us, and it starts with compassion for our own suffering and that of others.

To honor the magical way in which the book seemed to flow to me and stay true to my intention to share our real-life experiences, the writing that came forth to me was left in its original form, with minimal editing. In this way, the book feels like Katlyn—raw, unedited, and perfect in her imperfection. Like a live, unplugged musical performance, this is the purest expression I could offer. I also wrote the book in simple, conversational language in hopes that any literate person could comfortably understand the information presented. Because of these decisions, I may not have done adequate justice to the important subject material or the wonderful references I relied upon throughout the book. For these shortcomings and others of which I am not aware, as my mother would say when acknowledging a mistake, *I hope you can find it in your heart to forgive me.*

I want to offer my gratitude for your willingness to take this difficult journey with me, and hope that the life lessons offered in this book help you to find any healing you may need. May the principles and practices in the book also help you find greater happiness, well-being, and peace of mind. We all deserve this. Please accept my limitations as a teacher and a writer, and know that if not for the wisdom that flowed to me from another source, this book would not have been possible. Even so, I believe there will always be greater wisdom and truths to come. This book represents the best I could do for now. My intention is to keep on learning and growing, and my hope is that you do the same. The world needs us all to become the best version of ourselves that we can be.

Thank you also for respecting my feeling of connection to Katlyn and allowing me to offer her words here. I realize that for many, the idea that Katlyn could communicate with me after death is unbelievable. For those who share this doubt, you may be encouraged to know that my wife and I also retain a healthy self-doubt about this. We respectfully refer to Katlyn's words as *the hypothetical Katlyn voice* and allow ourselves to believe in *the voice* only if it makes common sense and helps us become better persons. We also have a cautionary saying about making sure we don't inadvertently get onboard *the crazy train,* so we recognize the need for healthy skepticism and the importance of not taking ourselves too seriously.

Of course, there is no way to know for sure if *the voice* is really Katlyn communicating from the other side, and likewise no way to prove that it is not. Even if my subconscious mind has fabricated Katlyn's voice out of my deep love for her and my intense desire to reconnect with her, I would still not change a thing. With that being said, I have presented Katlyn's words here because they are undeniably real to me, in spite of my healthy self-doubt. The truth is, over the last year Katlyn has come back to life for me in ways that my words could never convey. Please accept this as my truth and know that I am eternally grateful to God for this miracle of Katlyn's return to my life, no matter how this has happened.

After Katlyn's death, I played a song called *The Water is Wide* over and over again, each time crying hard for my loss. The words in part are:

The water is wide,
I can't cross over,
And neither have I wings to fly.
Build me a boat,
That can carry two,
And both shall row, my love and I.

Ninety days after Katlyn passed, after listening to this song and crying once again, I wrote the following words in my journal:

This book is my boat.
My heart is my boat.
My life is my boat.
Now I live it for two.
But both shall row, my love and I.

Though I didn't know it for sure at the time, these words have become my truth.

We cannot know for certain what awaits us after death. But by our thoughts and actions we can create heaven or hell while here on earth. Let us become the change we want to see, bring love where there is hate, and bring healing to ourselves and our brothers and sisters, thereby creating heaven here on earth.

When the light of truth and love comes in, the darkness of deceit and hate cannot long remain. And as Katlyn said, *The love we need is within us, and love is just a choice that we need to keep making every day.*

Wishing you much love and many blessings.

Appendix: Practical Applications

For some, a limited discussion of practical applications of the *LAUGH* principles may be helpful. This section covers five potential applications; 1) Relationships, 2) Conflict, 3) Who and What to Follow, 4) Parenting, and 5) Teaching. My intention is to provide some high level thoughts on how to integrate the principles into real life situations. The discussion is quite general however, and therefore only an example of how we might view our own specific situations. It is intended to provide you with suggestions, and not direction, because we all need to determine that for ourselves.

Relationships: We all want to be liked by others. When others don't like us, it hurts. Even when someone likes us, if we want a deeper relationship than they do, it still hurts. Some of the younger generation has decided to avoid this pain by not liking anyone too much. They just hook up, have fun, and move on. While there is wisdom in not getting too attached at a young age, we also miss a lot when we avoid deeper personal connections with others, as this is what we really need inside.

Women, in general, are more sensitive to this need, being the child bearers and primary child rearers throughout our evolution. Men tend to be more focused on self-gratification and less aware of our deeper needs for connection. This should not surprise us, as we can plainly see these general differences between males and females in the animal kingdom as well. Therefore, women have an opportunity to influence relationships by honoring their own wisdom and showing men the benefits of a loving connection. With such awareness, women can make choices that help create deeper connections and better relationships. This is not meant to excuse men from their own responsibility for creating deeper, loving relationships, it simply recognizes that women may have a greater awareness and power in this regard.

Aside from our tendency to avoid deeper connections out of fear, the other issues we discussed that most hurt our relationships are our expectations of others, blame and guilt, and the inability to listen. Having too many expectations of others, as discussed earlier, can be a serious problem for relationships. We are right to expect a certain level of acceptable behavior from others, for example honesty and respect, and there are relationships where such things are not present and should be insisted upon. However, any expectations beyond such basic behavior standards should come from mutual agreement.

For example, if we expect our friend or lover to respond to our specific needs of the moment without asking them directly and getting their agreement, this may be unrealistic and unhelpful. We may be particularly insecure and needy, and place too big a burden on our friends, families, or partners for love and attention. We also know that trying to change others is a losing cause. People change only from their own awareness and desire. When we are pushed to change by others, we are more likely to resist. Positive reinforcement is a more effective motivator. So, we could try to recognize our own neediness and undertake the work of self-healing when appropriate. Then we can accept others as they are unless there are basic behavioral issues that need to be addressed, as mentioned previously.

We could also be using our expectations to control and manipulate others to get what we want from them. We can make others feel guilty when they don't live up to them. Alternatively, our minds can become dominated by questions of, *What should I do?* to meet the expectations of others in order to gain their love and acceptance. We can live in constant fear of disappointing others. This starts for us as children and continues into adulthood. Until we come to self-love and acceptance, we can be easily manipulated by others and their expectations. When we allow ourselves to be manipulated, we usually behave in the same way toward others; that is, we try to manipulate them as well. This type of conditional love is a shaky foundation for a relationship that often leads to dishonesty.

Once we learn to love, accept, and honor ourselves as we are, along with our normal human desires and imperfections, we can live in our truth and let others do the same. Our self-esteem does not depend upon the approval of others. This is when honesty comes naturally. With self-love and acceptance, there is no more need for dishonesty, as we have nothing to hide. Then our relationships have a strong foundation to build upon. When we are dishonest out of fear of judgment, it is a clear sign that we need to work on self-love and acceptance in order to honor ourselves and have healthy relationships.

When we blame others for our problems, two dynamics come into play that are also damaging for a relationship. First, we stop taking responsibility. We assume the victim role, so our ability to resolve relationship issues greatly diminishes in that we expect only the other person to change. There's a bible verse from Matthew where Jesus speaks about how easily we point out other's faults while ignoring our own, *Why do you see the speck that is in your brother's eye, but do not notice the log that is in your own eye?* The other negative dynamic is that blame puts the other person on the defensive and makes it less likely they will accept any responsibility they may have. It's nearly impossible to look at our faults when we don't feel safe.

So, we need to let go of blame, and the flip side—guilt, as much as possible in order to maintain a healthy relationship.

Another skill that is essential to healthy relationships is the ability to listen. Most of us have an agenda, or something we are trying to get out of our relationships, and this can lead us to talk more than we listen. But our friend or partner needs to be heard and understood as well. When they speak, they are not normally looking for our ideas or advice. Therefore, we could try not to interrupt, but instead allow time for them to speak, to pause, to think some more, and finish their train of thought. Our patience and silence while they are speaking gives them the time and space to fully express themselves. It shows them our love and respect. *As the listener, less is always more.* That is, the less talking we do, the better it is for the person we are listening to. When they are finished, our best response is always an affirming statement to let them know we heard them, or a follow-up question to help them clarify their ideas and speak further, such as, "please say more about that." It takes a focused effort to be completely present with the person who is talking, let go of any agenda we may have, and just listen. But the quality of our relationships can greatly improve with such efforts.

Conflict: Generally, conflict arises when one party is not meeting the other person's expectations or when we fight over different beliefs. In more extreme cases, conflict can result in violence or emotional abuse. Although extreme conflict is not something we can effectively address here, the best response to emotional and physical threats is usually to try and stop it by withdrawing. When withdrawal is not an option, however, having the courage to stand up and fight for ourselves could literally save our life.

In less extreme cases of conflict, there are a couple of helpful principles to guide us. First, we should stand in our truth and not allow ourselves to be forced or intimidated into accepting something we don't believe is correct (except for threats of violence, where we should use our judgment to avoid physical harm.) As Shakespeare taught us, *This above all: to thine own self be true.* When we stand in our truth, we fulfill our highest duty to ourselves, which is to respect and honor who we are and what we believe. This also helps others because it effectively teaches them to respect and honor us as well, no matter how loudly they may protest. When we speak and live our truth, it sometimes causes others pain, especially if they are living in judgment of us or in denial of the truth. Still, we are responsible to live our truth and not responsible for the pain this causes others, so long as we don't neglect our legitimate duties and commitments to others such as our families, friends, and coworkers. And this applies only to speaking our truth and choosing to live by it, not to using our truth to justify any type of judgment or aggression toward those with whom we disagree.

A second guideline is that negative emotion is usually not helpful. When we use a raised voice or inflammatory words, the other person feels threatened and will most likely respond in kind. This escalates the conflict and does not help in finding a resolution. Although we may need to feel enough anger to stand up for ourselves and just say, *Stop!* to someone who is being abusive, for example, in most cases we should not raise our voice or vent anger on others. As the word implies, expressing our negative emotions puts our fears "in motion" in the form of an attack on others. This has the power to cause deep wounds, as previously discussed. When we feel such strong emotions, it is best to slow down, take some deep breaths, and wait until the emotion subsides before speaking. When others vent their negative emotions on us, we could recognize they are feeling threatened and try not to take it personally and react.

Earlier we discussed that our insecurities can manifest either passively or aggressively. When one or both parties to a conflict are aggressive, it's difficult to reach a resolution. If another party behaves this way, we could try to adopt a neutral or passive stance if possible. However, without a similar change in the aggressive party, it will be difficult to make any progress. Over time, both parties need to move away from an aggressive posture of anger or blame in order to develop a mutually satisfactory resolution. This may require one or both parties to seek counseling. Use of joint therapy or a mediator could also be helpful. It's better to recognize these troubling dynamics sooner and take corrective action before the conflict worsens. No matter how bad things are, we can always make them worse. At the same time, it is often within our power to make them better if we take responsibility for doing so.

Again, during any verbal conflict we should try to stay calm, and if we can't, we should step away until we are able. When we respond with anger and emotion, it is because we feel threatened. Although this is an instinctive defensive response that is difficult to control, we could instead try to see the other person as wounded and choose compassion. This is possible only when we don't take others actions personally. We could also recognize that our emotional response to perceived injustice is reflective of our own fears, regardless of what has happened. And if negative emotions arise in a relationship that's important to us, we should try to remember that to heal emotional wounds, the person needs to feel safe (don't shout back at them), they need to feel compassion (listen and let them know you care), and they need to find a way to get what they need (show them you will work toward a solution).

The best approach to verbal conflict, then, would be to listen with an open mind until the other person is done, even if their voice is raised. (Of course, repetitive emotional abuse is something different that needs to be addressed, as previously discussed). We don't need to ask questions other than to make sure we understand them. We could choose not to defend ourselves or point out where they may be at fault, at least not initially, because we need to accept their truth for them to feel safe. Once we have mutual trust, we can present our own ideas and work together toward better understanding and a resolution. In general, we should try not to run away from human conflict. Conflict presents an opportunity to stretch ourselves, grow in compassion and understanding, and learn that we are more capable than we thought. When we constructively resolve conflicts, our relationships often grow stronger. We are all better off when we learn how to work through conflicts. This should be our goal unless there is an immediate threat, as mentioned earlier, or the conflict is not resolvable.

In some relationships, conflict becomes repetitive. In such situations, we need to assess our own role and ask what our expectations are and if we are being the aggressor. Aggression and emotion is a sign that we have our own healing work to do. We are correct, however, to calmly stand up for ourselves and ask for what we need, which may be something as basic as kindness or respect. When we make our best efforts, but are unable to work through conflicts, or when we conclude that a relationship is fundamentally unhealthy and not likely to change, the best approach is usually to withdraw. In cases where the unresolved conflict or unhealthy relationship occurs with a family member, roommate, or coworker, for example, withdrawal may not be an easy option. When we must continue to interact with such a person, the best approach is to remain non-confrontational, try to minimize our interactions, and then try to diffuse any conflict that may occur. Over time, it may be best to remove ourselves from such situations, but in the short run we could try our best not to make the situation worse.

Lastly, even though we all want to be right, we need to realize we cannot be objective about anything, especially ourselves. We think we know "the truth" and that our truth should be self-evident to everyone else. But science has shown that none of us know the whole truth and that we all have biases in favor of our own opinions and huge blind spots regarding our own faults. We need to ask, "What's my own agenda?" because we tend to be self-serving and neglect to consider the other persons wants and needs. So we should do our best to keep an open mind, which starts with an open heart, respect for others, and some degree of humility. Additionally, it is normally best not to offer advice to anyone but our children unless we are asked. As Gandhi said, *Be the change that you want to see.* We best lead by our example.

Who and What to Follow: When we seek to become more loving, accepting, and understanding, it helps to associate with friends, teachers, leaders, and institutions that are like-minded. To do so, we need to discern the motivations of others. In general, we can always ask two questions: Are they 1) loving, and 2) accepting? Another relevant question is: Are they positive and life affirming or negative? Lastly we could ask: Are they interested in my well-being or primarily themselves? For example, most of the advertisements we see are from companies interested primarily in making money, not our well-being.

Another indication of positive people or institutions is they are open-minded and are not trying to control us in any way. A good example would be a school where they teach us multiple viewpoints to help us gain a greater understanding of basic truths so we can apply those truths for ourselves. In this way, they help us to graduate as independent minded and fully functional individuals. By contrast, if we look at some churches or political parties, for example, they repeatedly teach us the same simple ideas and have strict rules for our behavior. We are told exactly how to apply their truths and anyone that does not adhere to their teachings is wrong or evil. Like individuals, they have self-serving biases and can't see their own faults.

Unlike a good school, negative institutions don't teach higher truths and are not open to new ideas or questions. They want to keep us stuck in their school. Such organizations are threatened by our independent thoughts and any idea of our "graduation" because they need followers to stay in power. For example, to the skilled therapist, the thought that, *I am bad or unworthy,* is the core problem that needs to be corrected. For many churches, however, that same thought is what sustains them because it allows them to control us with guilt and shame. If we accept ourselves as we are and and let go of guilt and shame, they no longer have any control over us. This is when they define us as evil, even if our hearts are filled with love and innocence.

For most everything that is being sold to us, from material goods and services, to beliefs and causes, the "sellers" need us much more than we need them. The way to change our world, then is to change ourselves and stop buying into what harms us. For example, a politician who fights for the interest of a narrow constituency is not working for our collective best interests, which is their most important job. Most are primarily after their own self-interests, which is staying in power, which means raising more money and catering to the wealthy and powerful. We should look for open-minded candidates that are not selling us a narrow agenda, but are instead interested in working collaboratively with all parties to find solutions that best serve our collective interests.

Another example is how food and drug companies sell us products that may harm us, all in the interest of money. For example, the negative health consequences of eating highly processed and sweetened foods is well documented. But this type of food still fills the majority of shelf space at our supermarkets and the majority of menus at our fast food restaurants. Less obvious are the dangers of drugs like pain relievers and antidepressants. While most everyone in the pharmaceutical and medical communities will praise their benefits, there are clear dangers that we rarely hear. First, they are not curative. They only alleviate symptoms. Next, because they alleviate the symptoms, we are less likely to get the help we need. Next, without getting the help we need, the underlying problem is more likely to get worse. Finally, these drugs are addictive and have terrible side effects, such as making people irrational and suicidal, particularly those who are young and most vulnerable.

Imagine if the doctor or drug advertisement said, *If you take this antidepressant drug, it will only mask your pain, so you are less likely to get the therapeutic help you need, and your underlying depression is more likely to get worse, and therefore you may be more likely to kill yourself, because the drug can also make you confused.* They don't say such things, not because they are untrue, but because they are primarily interested in making money, not helping us. We have seen this before when tobacco companies were finally forced to put this type of warning on addictive cigarettes after millions of deaths and decades of denial and resistance. The drug companies and doctors that sell and prescribe equally dangerous and addictive medications as if they were aspirin taken for a headache, without adequate warnings or concern for curative treatment such as therapy, are really no different. They relieve our pain for money and don't seem to care if we are ultimately worse off. We need to ask ourselves, do we really want to change our brain chemistry to block out our pain instead of looking at our underlying problems?

Dr. Bessel van der Kolk, the Harvard trained psychiatrist who wrote the previously mentioned book, *The Body Keeps the Score,* states the following regarding the risk of antidepression medication; *Psychiatric medications have a serious downside, as they may deflect attention from dealing with the underlying issue. Instead, even as antidepressant use continues to increase, it has not made a dent in hospital admissions for depression. The number of people treated for depression has tripled over the past two decades, and one in ten Americans now takes antidepressants.*

So we need to realize that our governments are not going to protect us from profit driven food, drug, and healthcare companies and instead learn to think for ourselves. This applies to many other institutions as well because our world is driven primarily by people who are out for themselves, happily satisfying their own egos at our expense. Most of our leaders are the same in this regard, though they claim differently. When we buy into them to satisfy our own egos or our desire for convenience, we perpetuate the problem. But we have the power to change our world by becoming more aware, changing ourselves, and making more positive choices. Studies estimate that it would take less than 10% of us to make different choices in order to cause a major shift in the institutions that control our world. This seems credible, as elections are usually decided by smaller margins and companies that lost 10% of revenues would undergo major shifts. For me, 10% is also an encouragingly small number, particularly since all it takes for us to change individually is greater awareness and understanding.

We also need to be careful about where we look for help and advice. Our need for a safe and non-judgmental place to open up can work against us. When we have problems, we tend to discuss them with our best friends or family because this is where we feel safest. But they may have no understanding of what we are going through or what we need. And because they often share our fears and insecurities, they may not be well equipped to offer a different way of seeing things. We feel too ashamed to expose our insecurities to someone who we don't know as well or perceive as stronger, even though they may be more able to help. So we can end up with the blind leading the blind, or become frustrated with the lack of compassion and understanding among existing friends and family. Therefore, even though we need to find a non-judgmental and safe place to open up, and a trusted family member or friend is normally where we find this, we also we need courage to seek outside help when our needs exceed the capabilities of our circle of family and friends.

When we do look for outside help, however, we also need to recognize that mental healthcare practitioners have a wide range of capabilities as well. Some go into such work because of a personal history of psychological challenges, the effects from which may impact their competency as therapists. Additionally, like drug companies, some therapists may not be motivated to see us get well because once we do, we no longer need them. And when we are emotionally wounded and vulnerable, which is the point where we are most likely to seek therapeutic help, we are not in the best position to critically assess the competence of our therapist. As a result, therapeutic experiences are sometimes not helpful and can even make our situation worse. My own practice now is to never use a doctor or therapist without a strong recommendation from someone I know and trust. There are also rating systems for healthcare professionals available online. Lastly, I trust my gut instinct. If the person who is helping me is not someone I feel completely comfortable with and respect, I find someone else.

Parenting: There are many difficulties in being parents today. First, we receive little if any training other than observing the way we were parented, which may not have been the best example. Our world today is also much more complex than when we were children. The demands on our lives and the negative influences on our children have increased dramatically. Most families today have two working parents, driven by the financial realities of our time. Because of this, our children spend far more time out of their parent's sight and under the influence of others. Therefore, one of our most important duties is to do our best to ensure the influences on our children are positive.

When we are with our children, our primary duty as parents is to be loving and kind, even when our children are not. Love is what they need most, just like a baby. Because the world is unsafe, they need to feel safe with us. Life can be scary and relating to parents should not add to a child's fears. When our child makes a mistake, we need to correct them by showing them the negative consequences of their actions. But we should not express anger or negative emotions toward them, call them "bad," or make them feel unworthy, as this is deeply damaging to them. We all make mistakes. When we make a mistake as their parent, we should acknowledge and correct the mistake, just as we would want them to do. Then our kind and responsible example as parents becomes their teacher. We may need self-healing to meet these parenting ideals, but this is what our children need most.

One of the most important ways we show our children love and kindness is to listen to them and honor their feelings. We easily forget how difficult and confusing it can be as a child and often rush to tell them what to do, instead of first asking them about what they are thinking or feeling. As parents, we think we know what they need, but they may be struggling in a way we have not anticipated, as we are all different. And even if we do understand where they are coming from, our children still benefit greatly when we first ask questions to ensure all of their thoughts and feelings are heard. When we listen without interruption or judgment, we show them they are safe and teach them how to constructively communicate their thoughts and feelings (and by our example, how to listen to others). This skill, which is so important to all human relationships, is best learned from our parents.

Even if we actively listen to our children, there may be times when our child is struggling and won't talk to us. When they keep their struggles to themselves, however, there is real danger. In these cases, it's important that they have someone positive to talk with. A teacher, older friend, counselor or professional therapist may be good options. As parents, we cannot force our children to talk to us, but we can try to ensure someone is available for them. This is critically important once children approach their teenage years, when their hormones and peer pressures can cause them to feel extreme anxiety. Again, we want to ensure that whoever they talk to is a positive influence.

Finally, because our children are likely to face more negative influences than we did, they may need more skills than we learned as parents. This can pose a big challenge. Because children today often have much less adult supervision, they need to learn to self-regulate their behavior and approach situations from a place of self-awareness and empowerment. How can we help them as parents when we have not developed such skills? In these situations, the key is to recognize that our children may need more than we can offer and get them professional help when their needs are beyond our understanding or capabilities. This requires at least a minimal level of awareness and some humility. After giving our children unconditional love, listening to them, and trying to ensure they are around positive influences, our most important role as parents is to recognize when our children need outside help and get it for them, as they are unlikely to seek such help on their own.

Teaching: Teaching the best principles and practices to live by should be emphasized in our society, however, it clearly is not. This has historically been the domain of religions, but they tend to focus on their own specific dogma and speak out against those that disagree, which is not conducive to our general well-being.

Governments have been reluctant to enter this arena, believing this to be the exclusive realm of parents and religion. Positive psychology is the first branch of science to reject this notion and make the case that we should teach skills that lead to happiness and well-being. There is sound research behind their methods, so the arguments against teaching such skills no longer make sense. Martin Seligman's book *Flourish*, mentioned earlier, has compelling examples of the power of what he calls *positive education* to improve the lives and well-being of students, parents, and teachers.

Seligman's work also demonstrates the power of identifying our particular strengths or virtues (what he calls *Signature Strengths*) and then working to find new applications for them in our lives. To that end, he has developed a Signature Strength exercise which, like the What-Went-Well exercise, has been shown to markedly lower depression and increase happiness months later. His approach was to develop a list of key positive principles or strengths to live by that lead to greater well-being (like the *LAUGH* principles in this book), then identify which of these strengths we already possess and focus efforts on putting our particular strengths into practice. We can take the Signature Strength test in his book *Flourish*, or at the website (www.authentichappiness.sas.upenn.edu). Interestingly, of the twenty-four principle virtues or strengths that he has identified, love and kindness, open-mindedness, humility, and gratitude are among them.

We could also make a strong case that teaching the *LAUGH* principles and practices in this book would improve our lives. There is research that demonstrates both the need for and the benefits of being more loving, accepting, understanding, grateful, and humble. We can readily see the power of practicing these virtues, both individually and collectively. Our best choice for ourselves and our children, then, is to act in our own self-interests by practicing and teaching positive principles for living. Asking the same from our family, friends, and leaders—for example, to be treated kindly and with respect—is a way of teaching them how to live and making our lives better at the same time. Eventually, such principles will likely be taught and practiced in most schools, as the evidence from science is compelling and the common sense of such an approach is hard to deny, once you divorce such teachings from the domain of any specific religion.

To that end, we plan to offer a teaching program for use with the *LAUGH* principles. The program will have six-modules, one for each of the five *LAUGH* principles and one for the Practice. Each module will be designed for a 50-minute class, and target 10 minutes for teaching, then a 10-minute exercise, followed by 30 minutes of group discussion about the exercise. Our goal is to create an experiential learning program with a minimum of lecture time. In this way, we hope to take advantage of the collective experience and wisdom of the group. Once the teaching program is complete and has been demonstrated to be effective, we plan to post it on our website www.fortheloveofkatlyn.com for anyone who would like to use it. We'll also update the program as we get feedback from users and find better teaching approaches or options.

References

The following is a list of articles, books, and research papers referenced in this book.

"The U-Bend of Life: Why, Beyond Middle Age, People Get Happier as they Get Older," *The Economist* (16 December 2010).

Pew Research Center, *The Global Religious Landscape* (18 December 2012). http://www.pewform.org/2012/12/18/global-religious-landscape-exec/

A. H. Maslow, "A Theory of Human Motivation," *Psychological Review*, no. 50 (1943): 370-396.

M. E. P. Seligman, *Flourish: A Visionary New Understanding of Happiness and Well-Being* (New York, NY: Free Press, 2011)

J. Bowker, *World Religions: The Great Faiths Explored and Explained* (New York, NY: DK Publishing, Inc., 2006, reprint edition)

V. S. Harrison, *Eastern Philosophy: The Basics* (Abington, Oxon: Routledge, 2013)

J. Haidt, *The Happiness Hypothesis: Finding Modern Truth in Ancient Wisdom* (New York, NY: Basic Books, 2006)

A. T. Beck, *Cognitive Therapy and the Emotional Disorders* (New York, NY: Penguin Group, 1979, 1st printing)

D. Harris, *10% Happier: How I Tamed the Voice in My Head, Reduced Stress Without Losing My Edge, and Found Self-Help That Actually Works – A True Story* (New York, NY: HarperCollins Publishers, 2014)

R. A. Friedman, "A Natural Fix for A.D.H.D," *The New York Times, SundayReview* section (2 November 2014)

M. K. Gandhi and M. Gandhi, *Autobiography: The Story of My Experiments with Truth* (BN Publishing, 2008, reprint edition)

B. Magee, *The Story of Thought: The Essential Guide to the History of Western Philosophy* (London; DK Publishing, Inc., 1998)

E. N. Carlson, "Overcoming the Barriers to Self-Knowledge: Mindfulness as a Path to Seeing Yourself as You Really Are," *Perspectives on Psychological Science*, 8 (2) (March 2013): 173-186.

G. Kriyananda, *The Spiritual Science of Kriya Yoga* (Chicago, IL: The Temple of Kriya Yoga, 1992, 4th edition)

P. Yogananda, *Man's Eternal Quest: Collected Talks and Essays on Realizing God in Daily Life, Volume 1* (Los Angeles, CA: Self-Realization Fellowship, 1982)

P. Moffitt, *Dancing with Life: Buddhist Insights for Finding Meaning and Joy in the Face of Suffering* (New York, NY: Rodale, 2008)

S. Salzberg, *Loving-Kindness: The Revolutionary Art of Happiness* (Boston, MA: Shambhala Publications, 1995)

D. L. Kirp, "Make School a Democracy," *The New York Times, SundayReview* section (1 March 2015)

T. Koch, "What's Worse than Sad," *The New York Times, SundayReview* section (25 January 2015)

S. Cope, *The Great Work of Your Life: A Guide for the Journey to Your True Calling* (New York: Bantam Books, 2012)

N. R. Mandela, *Long Walk to Freedom: The Autobiography of Nelson Mandela* (USA: Back Bay Books, 1995)

J. C. Collins and J. I. Porras, *Built to Last: Successful Habits of Visionary Companies* (New York, NY: HarperBusiness, 1994)

J. Collins, *Good to Great: Why Some Companies Make the Leap... and Others Don't* (New York, NY: HarperBusiness, 2001)

D. Buettner, *The Blue Zones: 9 Lessons for Living Longer, from the People Who've Lived the Longest* (Washington, D.C.: National Geographic Society, 2012, 2nd edition)

E. Carpenter, *Life, Reinvented: A Guide to Healing from Sexual Trauma for Survivors and Loved Ones* (Denver, CO: Quantum Publishing Group, 2014)

E. S. Shneidman, N. L. Farberow, and R. E. Litman, *The Psychology of Suicide* (New York, Jason Aronson, Inc., 1983)

J. Herman, *Trauma and Recovery: The Aftermath of Violence—From Domestic Abuse to Political Terror* (New York, NY: Basic Books, 1992, 1997)

B. A. van der Kolk, *The Body Keeps the Score: Brain, Mind, and Body in the Healing of Trauma* (New York, NY: Viking, 2014)

Made in the USA
Middletown, DE
19 February 2016